Our Growing FAMILY

JOANNE and
RUDY SHEPTOCK

with

Wynelle B. Gardner

LOGOS INTERNATIONAL
PLAINFIELD, NEW JERSEY

Unless otherwise noted as KJV (King James Version), all Scripture references are taken from the New American Standard Bible, copyright The Lockman Foundation, 1960, 1962, 1963, 1968, 1971, 1972, 1973, 1975, published by Creation House, Carol Stream, Illinois.

OUR GROWING FAMILY
Copyright © 1979 by Logos International
All rights reserved
Printed in the United States of America
Library of Congress Catalog Card Number: 79-65214
International Standard Book Number: 0-88270-385-4
Logos International, Plainfield, New Jersey

Contents

Foreword   **v**
1 A Christmas Baby   **1**
2 Journey West   **13**
3 A Nun's Veil   **21**
4 Joanne's Meditations   **35**
5 The Exit   **43**
6 A Nurse's Cap   **49**
7 New Life   **55**
8 The House Full of Children   **63**
9 Cook's Tour   **83**
10 Baker's Dozen   **95**
11 God's Provisions   **109**
12 Mary Grace   **123**
13 Be Patient With Me, Mommy   **131**
14 A Christmas Celebration   **147**
15 Love in Bloom   **169**

Foreword

"Everybody loves a baby," says an old-time song. It's true. A cuddly, newborn, satin-soft, pink bundle of squirms is easy to love. When a baby waves his arms, coos or smiles, our hearts melt. Who can resist such a one?

But there are little ones who don't inspire love so easily. They are the ones who are neither white nor black, the misbegotten, the deformed, the mistreated, ill-used, broken and bruised children—who will care for these?

The older child, lonely, forsaken, unlovely and incorrigible—who will comfort him?

Thinking of such children reminds one of newspaper ads of kittens and puppies in cunning poses, their soulful expressions saying, "Take me home."

Take me home, feed me, love me, give me a name.

Tend my lambs, the Master said.

Government and social agencies take care of the physical needs of such children temporarily, but governments can neither regulate nor legislate love. It can't be ordered in quantities.

Love is a fruit. It nourishes all who partake of it. A wise

king once said, "Many waters cannot quench love, nor will rivers overflow it" (Song of Sol. 8:7).

I know a place where love for children flows like a river. A place where love is poured out by the bucket. It is a house with many rooms, all furnished with love.

Joanne and Rudolph Sheptock and their twenty-three children live in a rambling, old house in Peapack, New Jersey. Eighteen of them are either biological or adopted. In addition, there are always those who come in temporarily. The Sheptocks have taken the hard-to-place children: the mongoloid, blind, lame, those with neurological impairments or missing limbs and also those of interracial backgrounds.

Joanne, tall, with flashing dark eyes and a wide smile is "mommy." She can usually be found holding one of the children, other little ones constantly surrounding her.

Her husband, Rudy, forty-five, is tall and angular, often seen wearing an old red football jersey with the number thirty-eight on it. The little boys hang around him for a while then dart away on business of their own.

How did all this come about? What sort of people have hearts big enough to give so much love to so many children?

Joanne Sheptock, forty, makes this quite clear in the very beginning.

"God has led us to do this. Nobody could do it on his own. A long time ago He said we should take anyone who came or was brought to the door and He'd provide for us. That's His promise. This story must show *God's provisions*. This is His house and these are His children. We couldn't possibly do it alone. There's no way!"

Foreword

For them every day is a faith-walk with God and a love affair with children.

Joanne said, "The children need love but there is no love without discipline. They have to learn that if they disobey they get punished but we love them still. That's the same way God works with us. How can there be blessing when we are disobedient?

"It hurts when you have to discipline a child and he reacts in anger. I cry at night sometimes because it seems as though the children have hated me for making them obey. God gives me forgiveness for them so, you see, we can't take credit for anything. All the credit, all the praise, all the glory goes to Him. I also give Him the heartaches too!"

There are bound to be heartaches when there are so many hearts involved. Sometimes the Sheptocks are ready to sign adoption papers for a foster child, only to find the natural parent has changed his mind. The child leaves, often against his will, to find his life torn apart again. That's heartache.

How do they keep up with so many children?

"By getting to know them," said Rudy. "No matter how many come and go, I know each one.

"And this house—we could never afford this place on our own. If I should say the house is mine it would crumble in a day. It's the Lord's house and I'm just running it. He says He will take care of everything we need and He does."

Even the walls speak of the Sheptocks' belief and purpose in life. In calligraphy on a pale blue wall of the dining room, Joanne has painted in large letters this verse from the Bible: "Let your light so shine before men, that they may see your good works, and glorify your Father which is in heaven" (Matt. 5:16 KJV).

A friend once wrote to them:

"Christians are always talking and writing about the Christian life like it really doesn't exist, but I've seen it in you. I've seen Christ living in you, not just glimpses as I've seen before in others, but in everyday, ordinary life all of the time. Please be encouraged and lifted up because God is showing His love and power through you and your family. What a lighthouse!"

It's more than a lighthouse. It's a greenhouse as well, for Joanne sees their variegated flock of white, black and interracial children as flowers.

"I felt God told me, *These are your flowers. When they grow you'll have a bouquet you're not ashamed to give to me.*"

Like flowers, they need tending and nurturing. Some of them are wild, having bloomed outside the garden wall. Little flowers, big flowers, all colors; they need a certain amount of pruning. Yes, it may be that these children are flowers and Joanne and Rudy are the gardeners.

Better gardeners one could not imagine. If it is true that the natural tendency of a plant is to grow toward its light source then the Sheptocks are just right as plant-keepers. The source they point their children to and the light which they themselves reflect is that of a living, loving God.

Parents need to release their children into God's care and to trust Him with them. Parents must be examples to their children, doing all God expects from them. If they do

Foreword

this, they will be able to rest in God's promises concerning their children.

Since these are extraordinary children they have special needs. In meeting those needs Joanne and Rudy certainly don't think of themselves as unusual people and in many ways they are quite ordinary.

"Let your light so shine before men. . . ."

What were they like before their light began to shine?

She was in a convent, young Joanne Tedesco, praying the rosary, the Our Father and the Hail Mary. The plainsong and the chant filled her mind but not her heart. She kept hearing faraway music. Then she received a new name, Sister Thérèse Madonna.

I believe that the name God had reserved for Joanne Tedesco and Sister Thérèse Madonna was the name of "mother." The music she could hear distantly was that of a child's cry. It was music that could only be heard with the soul. It was strong enough to lead her out of the convent and into a hospital for nurses' training. It carried her out of the hospital and into a house full of children.

Rudy was on a destroyer, visiting exotic foreign ports. Tonight at sea, tomorrow Gibraltar. Where would the long voyage end? It had started in a bake shop in Clifton, New Jersey.

He watched the stars at night, infinite sparks in an ocean of midnight blue—uncountable lights, God's lights.

"I used to talk to God at night, standing on the deck of the ship. I figured if God knew all the ins and outs of my life and could still put up with me, then life would have a way of working out. I decided to leave it all in His hands."

OUR GROWING FAMILY

We opened the family albums to see how the journey had gone. There they were, pictures of the children at all different ages like flowers pressed in a scrapbook.

There were pictures of Joanne and Rudy.

"Oh, there's mommy as a teen-ager. Let's see that one!"

"There's daddy standing on a ship."

The children squealed and crowded around, taking turns looking at the pictures of mommy in a nun's habit, in a nurse's uniform, in a wedding gown; and of daddy in a navy uniform.

I looked too, wondering how in the world their story could be told so that people would believe it. I wasn't even sure I could write about love such as this.

Seeking a leading from God, I turned, as I often do, to His Word. He graciously gave me the exact confirmation I needed by having me open to Isaiah 58 and there we all were.

My part was the first few lines:

Cry loudly, do not hold back;
Raise your voice like a trumpet. . . .

And their part:

Is this not the fast which I chose . . .
Is it not to divide your bread with the hungry,
And bring the homeless poor into the house;
When you see the naked, to cover him;
And not to hide yourself from your own flesh? . . .

Foreword

Then God's part:

Then you will take delight in the Lord,
And I will make you ride on the heights of the earth;
And I will feed you with the heritage of Jacob your father,
For the mouth of the Lord has spoken.

Joanne and Rudy Sheptock have faithfully shared their remembrances, anecdotes and tales of the children. Only occasionally was it necessary to draw on imagination to portray a scene.

Some of the chapters are Joanne's. Some are Rudy's. It's their story. Perhaps the music will inspire someone who has much love to give and doesn't know how to give it.

Here's how!

                              Wynelle Bennett Gardner

1

A Christmas Baby

It was Christmas Eve, 1969. Joanne and I and six children had just finished decorating the family tree that afternoon. Our six children, Rudy, Jr., Mary Ann, Mary Frances, Robert and two who were foster children at the time were giving it a final inspection. Their ages were eleven, nine, two eight-year-olds, seven and five. We were living in Cedar Knolls, New Jersey, and had been there for several years.

Joanne had redecorated the house and had some of her antiques and paintings downstairs where the tree was. I could hear her cautioning the children not to break anything. We had only recently started fixing up the house the way we had always wanted to. I was making a good salary as head custodian for the Morristown, New Jersey, school system and we were beginning to be a typical suburban family—collecting things.

Our yard and grounds were in topnotch shape and we did everything the other neighbors did—back yard barbecues, PTA meetings, living a good life, successful but in a rut. Like everyone else we were trying to keep up with the Joneses.

It should have been enough just to keep up with our growing family. Joanne was working full time as a nurse in the evening hours when I was at home with the children. The size of our family would vary depending on how many foster children we had at the time. Often the state agency for children would call, looking for a temporary home for someone.

In a way we felt obliged to do this, for in our back yard, nestled among the shrubs, was a statue of Mother Cabrini, patron saint of children. Joanne had gotten it from a convent that was moving from Morristown. We later read all about Mother Cabrini. She came to the United States in 1889 with a small group of sisters and established sixty-seven religious houses, one for each year of her life. She became a United States citizen and was the first American to be canonized.

We always laughed and said Mother Cabrini was looking after us from the garden. She might have been our guardian angel at that, for there was a time when a hurricane came through and all the houses around us were flooded and had serious problems but we had none at all. At two o'clock in the morning people from the neighborhood were running all around, trying to save things that were blowing away. Driveways washed out and basements flooded. The house next door had water halfway up the sliding doors on the patio. We stayed dry, not even a wet basement.

One of the neighbors asked, "How is it you kept dry and the rest of us got flooded? Turn Mother Cabrini around and let her protect us for a while!"

A Christmas Baby

Mother Cabrini seemed to have her eye on us for a good reason. I would never have dreamed then of the number of children who would find their way into our hearts and home in time to come.

Two days before this particular Christmas Eve, we had received a call from the Bureau of Children's Services. They had a little girl who'd been born the day before and they needed a place for her. The natural mother couldn't keep her and the hospital needed the room. Would we take her? Joanne and I talked it over.

"What do you think, Rudy?"

"I don't know, Joanne. I don't see how you can possibly manage to care for another child, especially a new baby. Let's think about it."

I walked outside that night in the cold, crisp December air. The sky was clear and I could see millions of stars above me. It was almost Christmas. Was there a special star shining there for someone? I looked at Mother Cabrini standing cold and alone in the garden. She looked very wise but had no words of wisdom for me.

I had this strange feeling that I was on board ship again as I was during 1950. My job on the destroyer *Stoddard* was that of a baker. I usually baked at night because cooks were always busy in the galleys in the day hours and it wasn't possible to spread out and bake large amounts of bread and cakes.

After I'd finished or while I was waiting for bread to rise I would go topside and look at the water and the stars and feel the silence all around me like a dark blue blanket.

Sometimes I'd stand at the rail for a long time, hearing

the soft swish of the waves, seeing the whitecaps looking like bits of broken-off clouds. I never looked upon this as a way of meditation but I guess it was. Standing there in the midnight hours I would talk to God. It was never a formal, churchy type of prayer. I just told Him all the things that had happened that day. Told Him some of the dreams I had. We really got acquainted during those night watches. I finally believed He knew my name.

The quiet darkness of my patio in New Jersey was a long way from the warm Mediterranean waters of long ago but I still felt I knew God in the same way. I just told Him what the problem was.

"God, I don't see how we can take one more child. I think Joanne wants to; she's so crazy about little kids, but I'm afraid it's too much for her. This is a newborn baby. What should we do?"

Right inside me I could feel God speaking in a way I'd never felt before. He told me He was looking for a birthplace for His Son but everybody kept saying, "No, no, no!"

Whatever you do for the least of these, I felt Him say, *you do for my Son. Do you have a stable I could put a newborn baby in?*

I ran back into the house and found Joanne.

"Joanne, you've got to call the Bureau of Children's Services and tell them we'll take the baby. God showed me He's looking for a place for Jesus to be born, only it's this little girl with one arm. Tell them we'll take her."

Joanne gave me a big hug and her face lit up like the family Christmas tree. She all but flew to the telephone.

Now here it was Christmas Eve and we were

A Christmas Baby

waiting for something more than Santa Claus. We were waiting for a new baby to arrive. We had told the children what was happening and that they'd have a special Christmas Eve gift. They were very excited and kept running to the door to see if she had arrived. Then they would run downstairs to touch all the decorations.

They hung up their stockings along the stairway leading downstairs and there was a lot of good-natured tussling and teasing going on.

Joanne and I were in the kitchen talking, planning and baking. She wanted to make some last-minute cookies to take to a friend on Christmas Day and I was helping her.

Things got very quiet downstairs and I went to see why. Parents have to investigate silence as well as noise. In our house silence was more a cause for alarm than noise.

I stood on the stairs looking down at the scene before me, one that would be repeated in many houses on our own street as well as across the nation. Six children sat in a circle in front of the Christmas tree. They had hung their stockings and now were reading a story.

It reminded me of a beautiful children's story about Christmas that I once read. It shows how our family feels about love and sharing, each one having something to give. It was all about animals who lived in a snowy woods—squirrels, chipmunks, deer, field mice, rabbits and birds who were decorating a fir tree in the forest for Christmas. The birds brought bits of colored string and shiny pieces of glass to dress the little fir. Squirrels brought part of their hoard of nuts; some gave of their sparse supply of food, bits of bread or berries to put on or under the tree.

One small, brown sparrow had nothing to bring because he couldn't fly, having an injured wing. He sat huddled in a lower branch of the tree for warmth, giving advice to the other animals as they worked.

One of the birds, a large, quarrelsome blue jay, didn't take his advice too kindly, going so far as to say it was meddlesome and calling attention to the fact that the sparrow had no gift to put on the tree.

The chattering animals became very quiet and listened to the jay screaming at the shivering sparrow. A rabbit tried to console the sparrow by saying they couldn't have decorated the tree half so well if their friend hadn't supervised. Other animals agreed. The jay, however, couldn't seem to stop criticizing his feathered friend and the unfortunate sparrow felt worse and worse. He chirped softly.

"What can I give to show that I want to celebrate Christmas? I want to be a part of this beautiful time."

He heard the wind sighing in his ear. "Give something of yourself. Give something of yourself."

"How can I do that?" murmured the sparrow. "I don't know how."

Then he had a remarkable idea. With his beak he reached under his left wing and pulled out a long, brownish gray feather.

"Here!" he chirped in triumph. "Take my feather to trim the tree."

A cheer went up from the assembly of animals and a snowbird flew up to the very top of the tree with the feather and wedged it into the branches. It was midnight and the animals never expected in all the world that they would be able to see a brownish feather on top of a dark green tree dusted with snowflakes. But at that moment a full moon sailed from behind a puffy cloud and sent a long, slender ray of light to illuminate the feather. It began to shine with the brightness of a star.

The animals cheered and sang a song that could be heard all through the woods. The surly blue jay flew away and never returned.

Joanne had come down to sit on the steps with me and we watched our children. I've never forgotten that Christmas Eve. I believe it was the beginning of a new life for us as we were about to take in a babe with only one arm—a sparrow with a broken wing.

Joanne sent the children upstairs to have a late lunch. We knew it would be another hour or more until our new baby arrived, as the hospital was several miles away, in another town.

Joanne put the cookies away and I washed up the utensils. The children hurried to the playroom again to look at the tree. Although it was still early afternoon, they had the lights turned on. It did look grand. Homemade decorations fashioned by the children at school, colored paper circles strung together hung over the branches. A slightly crooked star decorated the topmost branch, hung there by Rudy, Jr.

Joanne and I sat in the kitchen, drank cocoa and waited. She said to me, "Rudy, do you know why I can accept this little child who's deformed?"

I didn't know.

"It's because I've had to learn the hard way that everything and everybody isn't created perfect. You know I was always a perfectionist. If people weren't acceptable by my standards I couldn't warm up to them.

"When Robert was born with a bilateral cleft lip and no palate, it was a real blow. It took me a long time to deal with my feelings of guilt, insecurity and perfectionism that his handicap brought to the surface. It's made a whole lot of difference in my feelings toward everybody else. God has changed my attitudes and standards. Know what I mean?"

"I do. I also know it's taken a world of patience to see him through six operations but it's been worth it. Yes, we've learned that everybody needs love, and that it has to be unconditional."

Joanne gave me one of her famous hugs. She had the last word. "And you know something else? I believe God has rewarded Robert by giving him that beautiful singing voice. It's a gift from God!"

I agreed.

It was getting chillier so I went to turn up the thermostat. Joanne left to check once more on the clothes, bottles of formula and a bassinet she had made ready for our new guest. She had hardly left the room when I heard car wheels crunching on the driveway. I called her and yelled down to the children just as the doorbell rang. Standing there in the frosty air on this Christmas Eve were two young women from the children's bureau. One of them held a small, pink bundle in her arms. They came in and we could see the little form wrapped up in several blankets but we couldn't see her face.

A Christmas Baby

The women sat on the couch and unwrapped the baby with all the children crowding around to watch. Under the heavy blanket was a lighter receiving blanket that hugged the sleeping child. Joanne pulled back the cover and we saw a beautiful little girl, looking like a little Indian, with her red face and dark hair. Part of her left arm was missing. She was wearing a gown and diaper, all she had in the world. These were her swaddling clothes and this was our Christmas angel.

The girls all wanted to hold her but the boys shied away, watching intently from a corner of the couch. Then the boys got the small, cardboard bassinet from the dining room and Joanne laid the baby in it. When she whimpered, we talked to her and cuddled her. She was just three days old, born into a cold, unfriendly world.

The children took a long time to go to bed that night because they were so excited. We shooed them out of the kitchen after they had a bedtime snack. Robert cut up an apple and a half of a carrot to leave for Santa's reindeer; then the kids climbed the "wooden hill," as grandmother used to call the stairs. Joanne and I brought the Christmas gifts out of the closets and from under beds and stairways.

The next morning as I watched Joanne holding the baby and saw the eager faces of the other children gathered around, I thought of a stable scene two thousand years ago and I knew we had done the right thing. I thanked God for showing us what to do.

Not long after we had adopted Mary Margaret, Joanne and I were sitting on the patio in Cedar Knolls one warm spring evening. The children were all asleep. We got to talking about the time she was in the convent and I asked her why she liked the name "Mary" so much. She'd been so set on having that as part of the name for the other two girls, and now here was another Mary.

"When I was in the convent, Rudy, there was one special room in the Nazareth novitiate building where we went for study and programs or recreation. I remember it had two pianos in it and a statue of the Virgin Mary holding a wreath of flowers. I always liked to go there.

"The novitiate hall itself looked like an old fortress, with its brown brick, and round twin towers with conical roofs and tall spires at the front of the building. I liked to go in this room and sit near the niche where Mary's statue stood. That way I could look out the opposite window and watch the trees waving green leaves in the summer or showing bare boughs in the winter. I guess it helped me concentrate on heavenly thoughts!

"Anyway, I'd go there sometimes when I was alone and enjoy the stillness. Sometimes the room was so quiet that I could hear my own heartbeat. I would turn, feeling Our Lady's eyes upon me. I'd look up but she was always smiling at the roses in her hand. So I've just always thought that she was special. I also thought that if I prayed to her she would tell Jesus. I don't think I believed Jesus loved me enough to listen to me himself."

Sixteen years had gone by since that time but she remembered so many details.

She grinned at me rather shyly, "Can you understand what I'm trying to say, Rudy?"

I said, "Yes," hoping she'd go on with her story.

A Christmas Baby

"I thought she was the most beautiful Lady of all. The statue was so realistic you could see the folds in her blue dress and the soft draping of her white robe. Even her name was like music—Mary, Mary. My friend took a picture of me standing near her statue one day."

I expressed my surprise that they were allowed to take pictures, but she said they were.

"A sister took another picture of me when I was a postulant, standing in front of a statue of Our Lord. I remember it so well because the Sacred Heart was outside the deep blue of His robes. I'll show you those pictures sometime."

"Well, okay, but only if you let me show you the pictures of me and the French girls on the beach at Cannes."

"Oh, Rudy, you always try to make me think you had a girl in every port but I'll bet you didn't!"

I laughed and teased her a bit.

It was a Saturday night and Joanne didn't have to work at the hospital so we had time to talk. I got up and turned off the patio lights to keep the bugs away. Joanne filled up our iced tea glasses and I sloshed mine around a bit.

"Rudy, do you ever get the feeling that we should be doing something else? That you'd like to be doing something different?"

She didn't have to explain, for I knew exactly what she meant.

"Yes, I get that feeling pretty often these days. I don't know just how to describe it except to say that I feel sort of dissatisfied. Is that what you mean?"

"That's what I mean, honey. All we do here is what

everybody else does. We try to have the best lawn, the most flowers, the newest car, the biggest barbecues. We're too materialistic. I want something more out of life than that, don't you? What can we do about it?"

I couldn't give her a specific answer but we talked a long time that night about what our priorities in life ought to be. We began to make plans for a change in our lives. We were still young enough, thirty-two and thirty-seven, to find the idea of a change exciting. The plans didn't materialize for some time however.

2

Journey West

In December of 1971 our third son, Matthew, was born. That summer we sold the Cedar Knolls house and bought a twelve-foot trailer. With the six children we set out for Colorado. Why Colorado? We really didn't know, except we had friends who lived there and told us how beautiful it is. It was fun to think of buying a place out West where the air was clean and fresh, a country place where the kids could grow up. That's all we talked about the whole way out.

Even the long trip was a big event in our lives. We stayed in motels and swam in the pools, ate in restaurants and generally had a vacation—our first in twelve years.

Since our wedding, we had never taken a vacation and we hadn't even had a honeymoon. Needless to say, we enjoyed this precious time together.

We were watching the kids splash in the pool at the motel a couple of days before we were due to arrive in Colorado. Joanne was wearing a yellow bathing suit that looked great on her. I thought she was even prettier than she was on the day we got married. I reminded her of that happy event.

"Well, Joanne, I guess we'll have to call this our delayed

honeymoon. Is that okay with you?"

She laughed and kicked at a beach ball Robert had tossed her way.

"Sure, honey, I knew I'd get my honeymoon sooner or later. But we did have a day in New York, remember?"

Joanne took Mary Margaret and Matthew back to the room for a diaper change and a bottle and left me to my thoughts.

When Joanne and I were married, April 4, 1959, I was working the night shift at a postal terminal in Hoboken and she was still in nurse's training at St. Mary's Hospital in Passaic, New Jersey. Since we didn't have extra time off we went into New York City for dinner and to see a show. I would like to have taken her on a fancy honeymoon but it was not possible.

I remembered how pretty she had looked in her long white wedding gown with a veil. I always liked her in her white nurse's uniform because it made her hair and eyes show up so well, but she was a knockout in a wedding gown.

After the wedding we took a small apartment in Lyndhurst, New Jersey. Joanne hated to stay at home alone at night and many nights she'd beg me not to go to work. I couldn't do that, being the foreman, and she knew it.

One night I was getting dressed to go to work at eleven and Joanne kept begging me to stay home.

"Stay home tonight, Rudy."

"I can't, Joanne. It's too late. They wouldn't be able to get anyone to replace me. Besides, I'm the foreman and I have to be there."

Journey West

Partly in fun and partly serious, Joanne grabbed me and held onto my shirt, tearing a big hole in it as I pulled away. I knew I had to hurry and warm up the old junk I drove because it took a long time for it to start, so I ran out the door, falling over a stack of milk bottles that clattered and rolled down the steps. It sounded like a free-for-all was taking place.

I'd hardly gotten the bottles picked up when a policeman appeared and wanted to know what I thought I was doing. It seemed that a concerned neighbor across the street had called the police. He pulled me back into the house. Joanne was lying in bed, reading.

"Lady, do you want to press charges against this man?"

Joanne laughed. "What for? He's my husband!"

Soon after that we left Lyndhurst and got an apartment in Morristown.

I continued my reflective thinking as I watched the children swimming. I laughed, thinking of those early years and of that particular incident when my wife kept me out of jail. Eleven-year-old Mary Ann sat down beside me on the edge of the pool. The other children were splashing and swimming in the shallow end.

"What are you laughing at, daddy?"

I tousled her curly hair and made believe I was going to toss her in the pool.

"I was thinking about when your mommy and I got married thirteen years ago, honey. We had some good times."

"How old were you, daddy?"

"I was twenty-six and your mommy was twenty-one."

"Wasn't that kind of old to be getting married? I think eighteen would be a better age," said this wise, old maid of eleven.

"Honey, when I was eighteen I was still in the navy and your mom was still in the convent."

"Daddy, I wish you'd tell me about all the things you did at sea. And I've never heard mommy say much about what it was like to be a nun. I'd really like to hear it. Please?"

"I'll tell you one of these days, little one, but right now I'd like you to go give mom a hand with Matthew and Margy so we can eat dinner soon. I want to take another dip before we eat."

"Okay, I will. But don't forget you promised."

Mary Ann ran off, shaking the water out of her curls as she went. Mary Frances went with her to help with the babies.

The rest of our trip was spent sightseeing and relaxing. We got to Colorado, and moved into the house our friends had rented for us. Within three days I had a job with the Arapahoe County School District as a custodian. At the end of the first week I received a raise. Joanne decided she would go to work too so we could get ahead faster. We looked around at property and decided it would be best if we bought a small house, so we put a down payment on one and began to think about getting more furniture and collecting this and that.

Then Joanne found out she was pregnant and began to feel sick. Remembering how very sick she had been

Journey West

before Rudy, Jr. was born, I worried about how she would manage with the six other children at this time.

Before little Rudy was born she would come home from the hospital and lie on the floor and pray, "God, am I going to make it?"

The hardest part, she said, was night duty when she had to take care of the thirty or forty patients who were assigned to her and the aides. She'd care for one or two then run and be sick, tend to a couple more, then rush off and be sick again. I was afraid it would be too much for her this time, being away from family and friends.

Actually, we had to be honest with ourselves. We were about to do in Colorado just what we had done in New Jersey. Starting to accumulate things and think about how much money we could earn between us and what was the best part of town to live in—that's what we were doing. Nothing had changed as far as we could see, except the location.

One day, six weeks after we had left Cedar Knolls, I had a call from the Morristown School District, asking me to take my old job back as building and grounds supervisor. That made up our minds for us. We got our deposit back on the house, bought a fourteen-foot trailer, said good-by to our friends and packed up to leave.

With some pretty fast and steady driving we made it back to Jersey in three days. All together we had enjoyed a six-week vacation, one we would never have taken otherwise. It had been a good time, but now we had a serious problem—a big family and no place to live.

We arrived in Parsippany, New Jersey, a little after midnight and got a motel room. Next morning we called

OUR GROWING FAMILY

Joanne's cousins, Peter and Vera, to let them know we were back.

Peter said right away, "You're going to stay with us until you find a place to live." It was an answer to prayer!

We checked out of the motel after breakfast and started to their house. At the first red light I made an amazing discovery—I had no brakes on the trailer. No brakes! That could have happened anywhere along the way from Colorado, over the mountains and along the isolated stretches of highway but we'd made it home safely. Somebody was looking after us, that's for sure, and I don't think it was Mother Cabrini!

We moved in with Vera, Peter and Uncle Vincent, who made us all feel welcome. Joanne and I slept in the basement, the children upstairs.

Later on we bought an old house in Chester, New Jersey. It needed a lot of repairs, was on a dirt road, and had one tiny bathroom for eight people. You would have had to be desperate to move in but we did. In a matter of a few weeks we could hardly recognize the place. Joanne went to work redecorating and I painted and repaired. Eventually, we added two rooms and a bath and the place gradually began to feel like home.

Late in 1972, we adopted an interracial child, one-year-old Mary Christine. A few months later, in February of 1973, our daughter Mary Claire was born. Mary Elizabeth, a nine-year-old foster child, had arrived around the same time. Several months after Mary Claire's birth we adopted Eric, a five-year-old black boy. Now we had ten children.

A family from Georgia moved in across the street from

Journey West

us in September, 1974. They were Rollie and Merlyn Bevers and their five children, Tim, Angela, Tria, Kristin and Richard. Merlyn, the mother, was destined to play a very important part in our lives but we didn't know it then.

Joanne should tell you about Merlyn. I think she'd like that.

3

A Nun's Veil

I'd like nothing better than to talk about my friend Merlyn Bevers.

I remember the first day I met her. She and her husband had been in their new house across the street for several days, but I hadn't met her before because I really didn't have time to do much socializing with the neighbors. I was working forty hours a week at the hospital and taking care of the house and our ten children.

This one afternoon I was outside waiting for the kids to get off the bus as they came home from kindergarten. Merlyn was out there too. We introduced ourselves.

In her rich Georgia accent she said, "I've been wanting to meet the lady with all the children. Are you baby-sitting for this flock or running a nursery school?"

I laughed and told her they were all mine. Just then the children came up the road from the bus stop; they were Eric, our little black fellow, and Merlyn's little girl, Kristin, who was just his age. Being from the South, I wondered how she might feel about our interracial and black children.

OUR GROWING FAMILY

We hit it off right away—Merlyn, with her soft, gentle Southern ways, and I with my busy, energetic manner. I could see something special in her but I didn't know what it was. She was always so peaceful and full of joy. I wondered what it was all about.

Merlyn and I saw each other very little during the next few months but a bond of friendship was beginning to grow.

It was during these months that Rudy discovered a lump in his neck. He went to the doctor who said he needed to have an operation to have it taken out. It was probably benign, the doctor thought, but there was always that chance that it might be malignant so Rudy decided to have it removed.

One day before my husband was due to go into the hospital, Merlyn brought over a Bible and suggested that we read it. Not knowing at the time what a comfort it would be, I told Merlyn I didn't have time to read it but I appreciated her thoughtfulness. She had written in it, "All my love, Merlyn." I wondered how she could love us when she hardly knew us. I took the Bible and put it on my dresser in the bedroom and didn't have any desire to open it for a long while.

Rudy had the surgery and we were thrilled to find out the lump was benign. Merlyn and her family were over one evening visiting with us and she told me about a Bible study she was going to and asked me if I'd like to go with her.

"Merlyn, I haven't got time to go to a Bible study. I haven't got a minute to spare."

She looked so innocent and young sitting there in blue

A Nun's Veil

jeans and a plaid shirt, with short, brown, curly hair, but I knew she was almost my age. I knew she meant well too, and I didn't want to sound too harsh.

"Merlyn, I really do thank you for giving the Bible to us and I hope I can find time to read it. I'll think about your offer and let you know."

I doubted if I'd ever have enough free time for something like a Bible study and I also wondered if it would be proper to go. It was something I'd never done before.

The next time Merlyn came by she asked if I'd ever found time to look into the Bible. I told her, "I'm trying but right now it just looks impossible. I haven't taken time to study and meditate since I left the convent."

"Convent? I didn't know you'd been in a convent. Tell me about it. When was it? Why did you leave?"

Her questions came rushing out and I really wanted to answer them. First I got up and looked at the children playing in the yard to be sure they were okay. Before I could start telling her anything, Merlyn had more questions.

"How old were you, Joanne, when you went in and how did you happen to go? Did you feel a special calling from God?"

"Okay, Merlyn, I'll tell you all I can remember but it's been a long time. It was 1952, in fact, and I was fifteen years old.

"I'm trying to remember what led me into the convent and I'm not sure what it was. I was very shy as a teen-ager, believe it or not! I was one of the tallest girls in my class, somewhat overweight too, so I usually felt self-conscious in groups."

Merlyn nodded. "Go on."

"I know I always looked up to the priests and sisters in grammar school at St. Margaret's and at Bayley-Ellard High School in Madison, thinking that they were so much closer to God than I was. I always felt I would like to be a missionary in China and work with lots of children and then maybe I would be close to God too.

"The best way I could describe how I felt then was that I never felt 'at home' at home. Since grammar school, I guess I always wanted to be in the convent."

I looked at the clock. I didn't think I'd have much time to tell Merlyn anything else before I had to start dinner. She had more questions.

"Did your parents object to your going into the convent?"

"Did they ever! Any time the subject came up my father would get furious. He made me promise that I would go through two years of high school and then if I still wanted to go into the convent he would let me."

Merlyn and I talked for another half hour and she kept wanting to hear more, but I knew Rudy would soon be home. I had to cook dinner, feed the children and then go to work. I promised to finish the story another time.

When she left and I began to peel potatoes, of course I couldn't think of anything else. It had been so long since I'd thought about the convent years. I seemed to remember things so clearly that I wondered how it was possible that twenty years had gone by. I knew I had changed a lot since then. Those years might almost have belonged to another life, or even to another person. I

A Nun's Veil

thought about my parents.

My mother, bless her heart, had been determined not to be sad about my going. She was such a tiny little thing, only four feet eleven, with a round, sweet face. She always loved to sew and had made many pretty dresses for me and for my sister Jeanette, who was five years younger than I. At the farewell party she gave for me, inviting all the family and my best girl friends, I wore a pink taffeta dress with a long waistline which she had made, and my dad bought me a flower corsage.

I thought I might try to find the old albums with all the pictures of that time and show them to Rudy and Merlyn. They'd get a kick out of seeing the styles of the 1950s again. I remember how I used to wear my hair very short, set close to my head, with one little curl hanging down over my forehead. It would look funny today but it was the fashion then.

Rudy and the girls cleared the dishes away after dinner and I threw on my uniform and headed for the hospital. It was a long evening and the floor was quiet so I had more time to think about that remarkable year of 1952 when I was fifteen.

I remembered the going-in part very well. I was to enter the juniorate program of the Sisters of Charity of St. Elizabeth at Convent Station, New Jersey, not far from where we lived. My father had finally decided to let me go and I was so happy and excited to be there. My parents had accompanied me that first day and we walked around the grounds before we entered Mother Xavier Juniorate, the building that would be my home for the next two years. I had no idea what those years would hold for me but I felt sure this would be where I would spend the rest of my life.

I changed from my regular clothes to what would be my new dress. I was entering the juniorate where we wore white blouses with a small black bow on the collar and a black jumper. When we went out we would wear small, white hats that looked like bonnets.

My parents were waiting to take my clothing home. They would have liked to take me also but I didn't want to go. I wanted to be right where I was.

Deliberately, I put my garments into the brown bag sitting on the floor, folded the top together neatly and walked out to hand it to my mother. She was crying. My father stared at the floor as they stood there. I hugged them both and kissed them, then turned without a word and entered the new world of convent life. God seemed to be saying He was pleased and a quiet peace came over me.

Because my father hadn't let me enter the convent two years earlier I was now entering into the third year of the juniorate. Most of the girls my age had spent the two previous years here as freshmen and sophomores. I felt a bit awkward joining them in the junior year but I soon realized there were more important things to think about.

The sound of a bell brought me back to hospital surroundings. For a moment I had thought it was the vesper bell and I expected someone to say, "Miss Joanne, it is the time for prayer. Will you come?"

But it was the telephone ringing at my elbow in the nurse's station and I answered.

"Third floor, Sheptock speaking."

It was several minutes before I could shake the feeling

of being back in the convent, feeling excited and frightened, being fifteen and starting a new life. I began trying to sort it all out—the convent years, the nursing years, marriage and children. Was there a plan behind it all? I felt somehow that I was on the verge of finding out.

The next day while the children were at afternoon kindergarten, I went to the basement and dragged out an old box with pictures and souvenirs in it. There was the old black album with the pictures in it that I'd told Rudy about. I looked at it and the other things all afternoon between sorting clothes and ironing.

It was all there in the box—notes, scraps of paper, pictures and pamphlets describing the early history of the Sisters of Charity of which I became a part. I was sure Merlyn would find it all very interesting, especially the history of the order which traced its beginnings to St. Vincent de Paul of France during the early 1600s. The congregation was dedicated to nursing the poor in hospitals and to the teaching of children.

I made a note to read some of the history to Merlyn.

"The Council Meeting of the Sisters of Charity of Mount Saint Vincent, New York, on September 13, 1859, planted the seed of our glorious congregation . . . Sister Mary Xavier to take charge of the new Motherhouse in Newark."

The young Sister Mary Xavier was described as "young in years, but mature in prudence and solid piety." The old Colonel Ward Mansion on the corner of Washington and Bleeker streets, Newark, became the first motherhouse. In July, 1860, Mother Xavier, "with her cherished Carrara statue of Our Lady, brought her nine companions to their new home . . . called Saint Elizabeth." At her death in 1915, Mother Xavier's small community had "become 1400. Her parochial schools numbered eighty-three and her other varied institutions in total numbered twenty-four."

I wondered what it would have been like to be a part of the very beginning of something momentous like the establishing of a religious congregation. It was interesting to note that we juniorate sisters lived in the very home "in which Mother Xavier enkindled the beginning spark of the charity of Christ."

I had an opportunity to think more along those lines when I answered the doorbell next morning to find Merlyn standing there with chicken sandwiches and a hot coffee cake.

"I'm inviting myself to lunch, so I can hear the rest of the story!"

She helped me get the children ready for kindergarten and the two of us saw them off on the bus before we settled down to lunch. I fed Mary Claire in her highchair, washed her face and put her down for a nap. Matthew, Mary Christine and Mary Margaret were already napping.

It was September but very warm. I opened a window in the kitchen and Merlyn washed the lunch dishes. We talked while we worked. Then we took our cups of tea to the kitchen table.

Merlyn straightened her blue denim skirt and got comfortable. I admired her outfit.

Impatiently she said, "Joanne, never mind my outfit. Show me the pictures and tell me about the convent."

I showed her the picture of me in my black jumper and

little white hat and one of me as a postulant.

"I don't understand the terms, Joanne. First you said you were in the juniorate and then you were a postulant. The only word I'm familiar with is novice. When did you become a novice?"

"That's just before you're professed, Merlyn. First we were in the juniorate, but they don't even have that category any more. When I became a postulant, there were about sixty girls in my class. Out of that sixty maybe forty-five became professed sisters. Some of us had a lot of trouble adjusting to convent life. There were a couple of girls who were in their twenties, but most of us were only seventeen and eighteen when we were novices. These older girls always seemed more 'holy' to us, but I don't know if they made the adjustment as easily as the younger girls."

"Did you have lots of prayer time and contemplation? Tell me about your studies."

"Actually, Merlyn, the scholastic work wasn't a whole lot different from any high school. We had math, science and English with periods for silence and prayer. The discipline was very strict. We had to obey or expect punishment. I even remember Sister Evangela making me stand for an hour once during one of my classes because I was misbehaving. The music teacher wouldn't let us sneeze or cough; when we did, she sent us out of the room.

"In the novitiate I had calluses on my knees from kneeling. We often got up at five-thirty to pray. The prayers were formal and repetitious. I don't think I ever learned to talk to God in the manner of a daughter."

Merlyn smiled and I thought I saw a special spark in her eyes. I wondered what I'd said to bring that about. She was looking at more of the pictures. I thought I'd better tell her it wasn't all just study and prayer.

"We had recreation and took long walks. It was in the convent that I learned to appreciate what God has given us, no matter how simple or how small.

"We weren't completely cloistered because we could go into town if we needed to, to visit the dentist or shop for something. During the first two years our parents could visit us and we could go home in the summer."

"Did you have certain work you had to do, like chores or kitchen detail?"

"Oh, yes, we'd walk up the hill from the high school and wait on tables in the academy and college or clean up the dining halls. We weren't supposed to talk while we worked. Sometimes we ran errands for the older nuns and were glad to do it. We were supposed to show them lots of respect. Then there was choir; I always enjoyed that. It was a big choir and we sang in a lot of places. I was fascinated watching the sister who directed us, the way she waved her hands not just when she was directing but even when she talked. It was funny to watch her."

Merlyn and I continued to discuss and laugh about the pictures she had lined up in a row on the table.

"Now this one must have been when you were a postulant, I think you said. And you wore a black apron and cape over the black habit? I didn't know your hair was supposed to show."

"Yes, our hair showed under the little black lace caps we wore then. As novices our hair didn't show. We wore

A Nun's Veil

the starchy white square hats with a veil and no bow. When you were professed you wore the stiff, fluted white caps with a bow at the bottom. These were so stiff they left ridges in your face and cut off part of your side vision. It's a good thing all that has changed. The sisters are a lot less formal in their clothing today."

Merlyn wondered if I had any special friends among the novices and sisters.

"Many of my friends were those of my own particular class, but some of them were novices. Unfortunately, we couldn't spend much time together because, as a rule, novices weren't permitted to talk to postulants.

There was one nun though who took a special interest in me. She was Sister Julia Agnes, in charge of the juniorate. She would listen to my problems and read the poems I wrote or look at the paintings I did."

Merlyn began to toss out pictures from the box in a great hurry.

"Joanne, do you have any of the poems you wrote? I'd like to read them."

She picked up two small notebooks.

"They're not in there, Merlyn. I think the poems are in the basement somewhere. Those notebooks are just notes I made at retreat times. I always liked the retreats."

Merlyn didn't hear me, she was so busy looking through the black, loose-leaf notebooks. I left her reading my notes and went to check on the children and to see what time it was. When I came back she was still reading the notes with a faraway expression on her face. I commented about how engrossed she was.

"They can't be all that great, Merlyn. I've almost

forgotten what was in them."

She began to read aloud from some of the entries.

"Joanne, you ought to read these again. I marvel that you ever left the order, feeling the way you did. Have you still got the same fervor for God that you had then?"

"I still love God, Merlyn, but I don't have time for anything these days except doing my job and taking care of the children."

"Well, you ought to read these meditations and see what you used to have. I want to read them all when you're finished."

After I got home from work that night I went into the kitchen where I wouldn't disturb anyone and read the notes I'd made while on a retreat before I became a senior novice. It was a seven-day retreat and I'd titled the writings, "Joanne's Meditations from Father Redmond's Teachings," starting in February, 1956.

Sights and sounds of convent life came back to me there in the sleepy stillness of an autumn midnight as I remembered classmates I'd studied with, prayed with, cried and laughed with.

It was almost as if I were seeing a picture of myself come to life while I read the thoughts of the young girl who used to be me, eager to please Jesus but not quite understanding how.

A moving picture of scenes and events flashed across my mind that night. I saw the sacred shrines tucked away among the trees and shrubs, remembering particularly the Shrine of Our Lady of Fatima with the little lambs and the three kneeling children.

There was the Greek Theater and the Shakespearean

A Nun's Veil

Gardens, the procession of nuns of the Schola Cantorum on their way to sing at Holy Mass in the Holy Family Chapel.

From a timid young girl in the juniorate, I saw myself as a postulant, sitting in class facing the blackboard, watching sister write the words, "The general end of the Congregation is to promote the glory of God and the sanctification of its members by the observance of the simple vows of poverty, chastity and obedience."

Obedience—yes, I'd learned that. And as I read I saw that back then God was leading me, preparing me for now, but I had been blind to His grace, wearing a veil in more ways than one. So many things looked different to me now that I wanted to add new thoughts to my novitiate meditations. That was the beginning of a journey.

4

Joanne's Meditations

These meditations are not my thoughts today but they reflect how I felt at a younger age before I realized that God's love is special for all of us and that we don't merit His love; it is a true gift from Him. Then I only had hope, later I would have a sure knowledge of His plan for my life.

February 27, 1956:

Take a good look at your inner soul to see if you're what God expects you to be. Don't be afraid of what you'll see.

Do I have the same fervor now as I had when I first started?

God singled me out of millions of other souls to serve Him in this community.

Am I measuring up to the expectations of God?

Am I afraid to meet God even halfway? Afraid He'll ask too much of me?

Lord, give me the grace to see what you want of me and the courage to attempt it.

February 28, 1956:
People in the world are satisfied with little out of life. As long as they have the comforts of life they are satisfied.

We are creatures. There must be a source of our life and there must be an end. Why am I here? What was God's reason for creating me? God doesn't need me but still He shares His qualities with His creatures.

God knew me eternally. God loved me from the beginning. That's why I'm here.

He sees in me something that is lovable.

My intellect is always seeking truth.

My will is always seeking good.

My heart is always seeking love.

No creature will ever satisfy my longings.

My heart will be restless until it rests in Him.

February 28, 1956:   Evening
"You have not chosen me. I have chosen you."

I am loved by God with a special love. We are not worthy of a vocation. Why should we question our vocation when little trials come our way? We forget that the religious life is a very special calling by God who loves us in a special way.

Who is worthy? Our work is eternal. Whatever God wants, I want.

February 29, 1956:
If a religious measures up she receives a peace of

soul only God can give.

A religious must never get attached to things, whether small or large.

We must always keep our human appetites mortified.

To be perfect religious we must:
> Conform to the teaching
> Know the rules
> Love the rules
> Observe the rules

All the little crosses which are sent our way are sent to sanctify us.

See if there is anything in your life, any tendency to anything that would keep you from serving God as you should.

February 29, 1956:   Evening

Could I miss the end for which I was created?

Could I fail to reach my goal? Yes.

God created us all for heaven but we must merit the place God created for us.

He gave us a free will. We can say yes or no to anyone, even God.

He gave us a code to follow, the Ten Commandments.

God restricted us in some things to test our loyalty.

The world would justify sin by saying everybody's doing it.

St. Ignatius says to see ourselves in the presence of God, in our unatoned sin. Then picture God turning His back on us.

Where God is, sin can't be. Where sin is, God can't be.

March 2, 1956:
Obedience: Jesus came to Nazareth and He was subject to His parents. During His thirty years at Nazareth He was subject to obedience. He wanted us to understand the importance and holiness of obedience. We can't live peacefully without obedience.

Christ grew in wisdom and age and grace before men.

We are a part of His church and He wants us to play a good part. He wants us to have a sense of responsibility.

March 3, 1956:
Learn early to work, then our work will be for God.

Reverence the old and the sick.

There are two standards in the world: the standard of Christ and the standard of Satan. Learn to overcome Satan. He wants to plan a campaign to win souls from Christ.

He doesn't step up to a soul and entice the person to commit a mortal sin right away. He brings them along the way through something innocent. Gets them devoted to money, for example. Money can be innocent. It can be used for good purposes. After they're interested in money, they'll want to be somebody. They will crave earthly honors. Once he gets them that far he can develop pride in them and then they will think they're little gods and they won't need God.

Satan will tempt you in your weak areas. An indifference toward the rules, justifying any type of life, later on a disregard for life.

In the matter of curiosity about our reading material, he makes us believe it's for educational purposes.

The desire for popularity, yearning to be sought after—Satan will work around our predominant passions.

What is his approach to me?

March 3, 1956:

A few days away then we must rededicate ourselves as religious.

This is my life. We'll have our ups and downs but through it all if we mean this dedication we will receive the peace that comes from heaven.

This is my beloved daughter in whom I am well pleased. I am yours, dear Lord, and yours I wish to be.

Someday I'll be in heaven with Him (I hope).

Letters to Jesus

Dear Jesus:

Our first night is over. Gee, I'm kind of scared.

Please give me the grace to make a good retreat—really good.

I hope to be able to talk to father and straighten out so many things which have been bothering me for the longest time.

Give me the courage to really see my inner self and acknowledge all my faults.

I want to be able to want anything you want. Don't let me get too attached to things. Let me be able to go anyplace and love it, to be with anyone and love them.

I want to be a religious after your heart and no one else's.

I love you.

Joanne

Dear Jesus:

After Friday I don't think I'll ever be afraid again. Please help me to go through with it. With your grace I can do anything.

Please dear Jesus, I want to be a good novice, living my novitiate days and the rest of my life for you and only you.

I love you.

Joanne

Dear Jesus:

It's almost over. I can't wait until habit day. This retreat certainly has meant a lot to me.

I am now in a state of sanctifying grace, something I don't think I was in before the retreat. Please help me to stay that way always. I love you very much.

Sister Thérèse Madonna

Tis come at last, the blessed day
For which I long have sighed;
I am, O dare I say the word?

Joanne's Meditations

Jesus, I am thy bride.
Not all the powers of heaven or hell
Can tear me now from thee,
Can rob me of the right to call Thee mine eternally.
The cross, the beads, the holy veil, the habit that I wear,
Tell me to raise my thoughts to heaven for Jesus, thou art there!
And, O how sweet in life's last hour,
To think God's will I've done,
I've been obedient unto death, like His eternal Son.
(Author Unknown)

5

The Exit

    I lay awake a long time that night, hearing Rudy snore lightly beside me, thinking of what had come after the retreat and what had led me out of the convent. I was almost sorry Merlyn had brought up the subject because it made me think of things I'd long ago put away from me.

    More pictures came into my mind as I recalled Summer Festival which came to be Family and Friends Day each August when postulants, novices and professed sisters all enjoyed a free day on campus in an atmosphere of a miniature world's fair.

    In retrospect, I remember that I always watched the seasons change in the trees and flowers around the chapel. From summer green to gold and red in the fall, later to be covered with layers of snow that seemed to magnify the holy stillness of that place.

    Long halls, sometimes dark and musty, unexpected brightness in the statues and tapestries that lined some of the rooms—all this I reflected upon, all because my friend had said, "Tell me about the convent."

    Yes, I'd made my retreat and had become a novice. I

had received a new name, Sister Thérèse Madonna. Only a few more months to go and I would walk down the aisle, the "bride of Christ." I would be professed.

My parents came for habit day and brought me a beautiful purple orchid to wear. Now that I was a novice I wore the square, white hat with the veil. I recommitted myself to God and began to really feel a special calling. I listened more intently to the reading of Holy Scripture. One of my favorites was the story of Abraham and Sarah. By faith Abraham believed God as he stood with Sarah and heard God speak: "I will make you the father of a multitude of nations. Your descendants will be as the sands of the sea, as the stars of the heavens. Uncountable!"

I pictured Sarah as a bride in long robes of saffron, rose and desert gold. I imagined how she would have braided her long black hair and wrapped golden sashes about her waist. Sarah would have been beautiful even in her old age, even as she was about to become a mother.

"Why did you wait so long, God, to make her a mother?"

She was in training, God told me. She needed a multitude of years to equip her for the job God had in mind for her.

She would need patience, so God waited until she was ninety years old to give her a child. She would need courage to follow her husband through many miles of dangerous journeys. God reminded me that mothers are not made in an instant but require special molding and shaping.

Sometimes when I'd let my imagination run away with me I would confess this as sin, knowing that it kept me

The Exit

from centering my mind on holier things. If I were not given a difficult penance I would then set myself some punishment. Rising earlier, saying more prayers, giving up something, all these were ways I tried to become holier by doing my own thing.

In spite of my deep-seated fervor and love of God, I don't think I understood anything. I thought I had to be good enough on my own. I did learn to say yes and not to question God. I learned obedience but it wasn't enough to fill my heart.

Then I became very ill and no one could find out the reason why. I was a senior novice and should have been joyfully preparing to be professed within a few months. Instead, I went home to Morristown, New Jersey, very ill indeed.

That whole summer of 1956 I grew thin, hardly eating. I developed an abscess in my throat and had to spend three weeks in the hospital. My parents were very worried.

I prayed to God while I was in the hospital, trying to find out what I should do. There were times when I felt I couldn't really be me in the convent. And yet there were times when I felt that was where I belonged. There were so many things I couldn't come to grips with. I really loved people and needed to be with them. We were not supposed to become attached to anything, even people, for we were to give up material things and be ready to move at a moment's notice.

If I went back to the convent I would have to begin all over again. Finally, I decided to try again. God saw my heart was willing and they took me back.

But it was not to be. Slowly but surely, my heart was

telling me I didn't belong there. I thanked God for all He had shown me while I was in His care for four years, but in the end I left. Convent walls and a classroom were not to be my life. It was August, 1956. I was almost twenty.

The sisters were very nice to me. They counseled with me, trying to help me decide. Sister Julia Agnes, my very special friend, spoke to my mother, who often sewed habits for her and the other nuns.

"Mrs. Tedesco, Joanne's been away from home for four years. She will have a difficult time adjusting to this new way of life. Don't let her become idle, sitting around with nothing to do.

"Why don't you send her to St. Mary's Hospital in Passaic? I have a friend there who might help her get into their program for nurse's training. Will you think about that?"

My mother agreed. First, she arranged to send me on a short vacation to the Jersey shore at Long Branch with an aunt.

The summer shore wasn't the most peaceful place in the world to me. It was a little confusing. We went swimming and had many picnics. There were always people around. My cousins and some of the neighborhood young people would sit outside on the porch in the evening and talk about current happenings. I knew little of what was going on in the world but I listened anyway, scarcely understanding some of the expressions they used.

They all seemed to be crazy about dancing to rock'n'roll music and collected records by the dozens. They were always talking about new records.

"Hey, Patty, have you got Elvis's latest record?"

The Exit

"You bet! I really dig that 'Houn' Dawg'!"

Somebody else piped up, "Did you know Elvis Presley is going to give a concert in Asbury Park next month? Man, I'd give my eyeteeth for tickets to that!"

Finally, I couldn't stand it. I asked a girl sitting next to me, "Who is Elvis Presley?"

Everybody laughed as if I'd just asked if the world was square.

They all chimed in. "Where have you been? In jail?"

"You've got to be kidding. Everybody knows who Elvis Presley is."

"Yeah, he's the most!"

I felt foolish and a little angry. I got up and walked into the house. I knew my cousins would tell them. I always heard people whispering around me, "There's the girl who left the convent. There's the girl who left the convent. Wonder why she left?"

Back then it seemed like a sin to leave the convent. Now it happens all the time, but very few left in those days. It was very hard for me to adjust to people's attitudes. The transition from the quiet routine of St. Elizabeth's to the noisy, outside world was very difficult.

I kept thinking of what Sister Julia Agnes had said about nurse's training. Always shy, I wondered if I'd have the courage to begin something new. I dreaded having to find St. Mary's all by myself.

One day though, I got on the train at Morristown and rode to Passaic. We didn't have a car and my parents couldn't go with me. It wasn't like me to venture out on my own in that way and they were surprised by my boldness. So was I.

I found the hospital and located the nun who was a friend of Sister Julia Agnes. She was in charge of the nursing program.

We got along well and she asked me lots of questions.

"Do you like being with people, Miss Tedesco?"

"Yes, sister."

"Do you think you would like taking care of them? It's not always pleasant, you know. It would be a far cry from your life in the convent."

I nodded. "I think that's why I came out, sister. I want to be with people, helping them in whatever way I can *now*. I think I can do it."

They gave me an entrance test which I passed. In September I enrolled at St. Mary's, studying to become a nurse. I had been out of the convent less than a month.

Sister Julia Agnes had said, "Don't let her become idle." I think our whole family was glad that a new door had opened in my life. There was no way I could be idle and be a student nurse.

6

A Nurse's Cap

I had thought I would find it difficult studying the subjects I needed to become a nurse. I didn't, probably because I really had my heart set on learning everything I could but mostly because I couldn't stand the thought of failing again. I was in a hurry to go somewhere and the books, lab experiments and tests were the road that would take me there. I liked every day of it.

Some of the student nurses could think of little else but the handsome interns and the fascinating doctors we worked with every day. I was friendly with all of them but no special one caught my eye. I was really content to study and make good grades, anxious to graduate. That was September, 1956.

At St. Mary's we sometimes took a break in the hospital coffee shop. Whenever we could, we would go there and talk about the newest intern or what sort of grade we got in biology lab. Two of my girl friends and I had a special table where we sat and I always had the uncomfortable feeling that someone was watching me.

One day I looked up and saw the coffee shop manager

looking at me. He was tall, with dark hair and dark eyes; I thought he was quite nice-looking. He came over to our table on some pretext and spoke to a pretty blonde named Nancy. All the time he was talking to Nancy he was looking over her head at me. I hurried with my snack and went back to class. Later Nancy told me she had a date with him. He was nice, she said, and she liked him a lot.

My class wasn't so large but I soon realized that the tall, dark, coffee shop manager was dating girls right and left from our group. I finally asked someone what his name was and they told me he was Rudy Sheptock from Clifton. I decided to ignore him. If he wanted to take out every girl in our class, let him be a Casanova. It didn't matter to me. When the other girls would talk to him and get second cups of cocoa free or extra desserts, I kept my distance and refused his favors. For the longest while I didn't go near the coffee shop.

One day my friend Doris came to me and said, "Rudy Sheptock would like to have a date with you."

"You're crazy! I'm not going out with him!"

She insisted. "Listen, you can double-date with John and me. Just come this once."

Reluctant, I agreed.

It was raining very hard the day we decided to go out to dinner. We ate in a diner not far from the hospital, then we drove around town for a while and back to the nurses' quarters. I liked him a lot better than I had expected but still never considered going out with him again.

A few days later I was sick with the flu and couldn't get out of bed. I had a very high fever, sore throat and felt

A Nurse's Cap

miserable. About noon I heard a knock on the door and I called out, "I'm sick, but come in if you want to."

The door opened slowly and I couldn't see anybody standing there. I sat up and saw that the entire doorway was just about filled with flowers, with two legs underneath. This gigantic basket entered the room and a voice spoke out of the middle of it.

"These are for you, Joanne, and here are juice and sandwiches to go with them."

I recognized a friend's voice and asked her to read the card. I couldn't imagine who would be sending me all these things. She took the card off the red satin bow and read, "Get well soon. Love, Rudy."

I'd have fainted on the spot but I was afraid someone would think I was dead, for this had to be the biggest, floweriest, sweetest-smelling funeral basket I had ever seen!

My friend was giggling. "Joanne, it should have said, 'Deepest sympathy'!"

All afternoon I lay in bed and looked at the flowers, mostly gladioluses.

Now and then I would just laugh out loud, forgetting my sore throat. The fragrance was so overwhelming I finally put my head under the covers and went to sleep.

Later on, my roommate came in and just about died laughing. Of course she told everybody in class and they all began to tease Rudy.

One of Rudy's previous girlfriends came in to see me one afternoon. She asked how I felt and if I would soon be back in class.

"I'm feeling better, and I hope to be back in class soon.

OUR GROWING FAMILY

I'm sick of this bed. Four whole days stuck in here!"

"Your flowers are beautiful. You're really lucky."

"I know."

"Okay if I water them for you?"

"Why sure. That would be fine."

She got a water pitcher and filled it in the bathroom, then carefully poured water into the container set in the basket. I hoped she wouldn't spill water on her freshly-ironed, starchy, white uniform.

After she watered the flowers, she sat on my bed and said, "You should be very proud that someone like Rudy Sheptock likes you. He's a really nice guy. You may not know it but he doesn't only take out pretty girls like you, he takes out plain ones, too.

"At a party he'll dance with the girls nobody else will dance with. Did you know that?"

I shook my head no. She was answering a lot of my questions about this "Casanova."

"He doesn't want to get serious with anyone though, so he usually moves on to someone else if we start making noises like we're serious. He doesn't want to hurt anybody. He's probably the gentlest, most sincere, uncomplicated person I've ever met. He's the Sergeant York type, if you know what I mean."

I nodded and squeezed her hand. "Thanks for everything."

Rudy and I started going together on a steady basis after that. We both knew we didn't want to get married so we just enjoyed having dates, doing simple, inexpensive things. Lots of times we'd drive to a little club near Paterson that had a free jukebox. We'd dance for hours,

A Nurse's Cap

sharing pizza and Cokes.

I found out for myself that Rudy was a kind of hero type. He wouldn't compromise with what he believed. I began to admire him very much. It wasn't too long until my feelings went deeper than that. For a year we went together, getting to know each other. I was in my senior year of nurse's training and still not quite ready to get married, I thought.

Then one night we went to a movie, a Doris Day picture I think. It was a romantic musical. As always in those days, there was a happy ending with wedding bells. It was almost September and you could feel fall in the air. That night when Rudy took me home he asked me to marry him.

I said yes. We set our wedding date for April 4, 1959, a little over six months away. I would graduate from nursing school the following September, laying aside my bridal veil for a nurse's cap. I was twenty-one and Rudy was twenty-six.

Now, lying in bed beside my husband of fourteen years, I could hardly believe all the things that had happened to us since our marriage.

Instead of a nun, I was now a nurse. Instead of a missionary, I was now a mother with ten children.

God moves in mysterious ways, I thought.

"I wonder what's in store for us next?" I didn't realize I'd spoken out loud, but my question woke up Rudy.

7

New Life

I woke up when I heard Joanne's question, "I wonder what's in store for us next?"

I looked at the clock on the bedside table. Its shiny hands showed two-thirty in the morning.

"Joanne, for Pete's sake, why are you awake at this hour? Why are you talking out loud? I have to get up at six, you know."

She sighed and asked, "Do you remember when we got married, Rudy?"

"How could I forget? Of course I remember. But I know our anniversary isn't until April, dear, and this is only September. How come you're reminding me so early?"

"No special reason. I was just thinking of all the things that have happened to you and me the past sixteen years and was wondering what's in store for us next. I was thinking about the kids, all ten of them. Do you think we'll get to adopt Mary Elizabeth any time soon?"

"Go back to sleep, honey, and we'll talk about it in the morning. If we get too wide awake we'll never get to sleep again and I've got a rough day at school tomorrow. There are lots of problems to iron out this time of the year."

Pretty soon I heard Joanne's soft breathing and I must have fallen asleep again soon after. The next morning she seemed so quiet and introspective I wondered what was on her mind. I'd seen the pictures she had put out to show Merlyn and I guessed it had something to do with thinking about her convent days.

Also I wondered if the job at the hospital was getting to be too much for her. She'd talked me into letting her go back to nursing because we really needed the extra paycheck. She was at home in the daytime when I worked and I was at home while she worked the evening shift, so there was always somebody to look after the children. Once in a while she had to leave the children with a baby-sitter. I wondered now if she should have gone back to work after Mary Claire was born.

Then she told me a few days later that she was going to start attending a Bible study with our new neighbor, Merlyn Bevers. She went to this meeting on Thursday evenings for a few weeks.

She came home from Bible study one Thursday night and I was waiting for her in the kitchen. I'd made fresh coffee and had baked some doughnuts for the kids.

We sat down at the table, sampling the doughnuts. I was glad to see I hadn't lost my baking touch from my navy days, glad too that I was only baking for twelve instead of nearly two hundred.

I noticed Joanne seemed excited about something. She looked at me intently and said, "Rudy, I think I have had a revelation from the Holy Spirit because tonight I understood for the first time how the disciples were able

New Life

to leave everything they had and follow Jesus. Pastor Weber is the leader of the Bible study. You need to come with me and see these people. There's something different about them. It must have been Jesus I saw in the minister because I would have voluntarily gone with him to China if he had asked me to. I felt I could go anywhere for Him right then."

I looked at her calmly and said, "Fine. I'll come sometime."

The next week I went to the Bible study with Joanne. She was right; the people were different—so radiant and enthusiastic. Shortly after this, I noticed a definite change in her as well. She was forever smiling and humming, constantly listening to some Christian records she had bought.

Every time I was out in the yard I would see her talking with Merlyn. I wondered what they were always discussing. It was as though they had a secret. They never seemed to get tired of being together and talking. I guess I was beginning to not only wonder about their conversations, but I frankly felt left out and didn't know how to express my feelings.

I didn't know that Joanne had had a personal encounter with Jesus. All I knew was that I didn't feel so much a part of her life any more.

My curiosity got the best of me. One evening as we were getting ready for bed, I asked, "Tell me about Merlyn, Joanne. What do you and she talk about all the time?"

She gave me that wide, slow smile of hers that made her two dimples show up. I thought she was prettier than ever, still energetic and enthusiastic about everything.

I went on, "You both know a secret of some kind I think, because you act so differently and are together all the time. Tell me what it's all about."

"Rudy," Joanne explained, "remember how we both remarked that there was something special about Merlyn? How she's always quiet but seems about to burst out laughing and how she never gets riled up no matter how I let off steam and yell about things. I've never known anybody who has the kind of peace she has."

I nodded, agreeing with her. I liked Merlyn a lot but I hadn't let it bother me that I didn't have the qualities she seemed to possess. Apparently it had bothered Joanne.

She said, "Rudy, I think I've found what she's got."

I didn't know what to expect.

Joanne went over to the dresser and took out a small, yellow booklet.

"I don't know if you've seen the *Four Spiritual Laws* booklet Merlyn gave me."

She handed it to me. I'd never seen this particular kind but I had an idea of what it was like, just some religious tract. I gave it a glance or two. It was something that Campus Crusade for Christ uses to win converts. I handed it back to her.

"Rudy, this booklet explains what I failed to get ahold of when I was in the convent. It tells how God loves us and has a plan for our lives. The only thing we have to do to receive it is to believe in Jesus Christ. I used to think I had to earn all I got from God. I see now that nobody can earn it. It's free. I used to think I had to be good enough on my own to win God's favor. We can't add a thing to what He did. That's why Christ died and rose again. He took care of it."

I nodded again. I'd heard all that many times before in homilies and catechism. I was surprised Joanne found it so new. She went on.

"Well, the other night I just knelt by the bed and prayed these prayers. I asked Christ to take over my life. I asked God to show me what He wanted to do with my life."

Even with all the explanation, I still couldn't understand her absolute concentration on this new experience. I'd always wondered if Joanne wished she'd never left the convent. Maybe I thought she was somehow trying to get back or was substituting something else for it. I really didn't know what I thought but I was pretty upset and confused by her sudden religious excitement.

A month later I was convinced that Joanne didn't need me any more. Her friend listened to her problems. It was Easter Sunday and we'd just come home from church and were sitting outside by the picnic table, watching the kids hunt Easter eggs. The girls still had on their pretty, fluffy pink and blue dresses with matching socks. The boys' hair was combed and they wore light jackets and light-colored trousers. Joanne was afraid they would fall down and get grass stains on the knees. They were yelling and running all around the yard, hurrying over to show us what they found.

"Look, I found the blue egg with a gold cross on it. That wins the prize, you know!" Mary Frances ran over with her prize egg and put it on top of the others in the basket. Joanne had decided that whoever found the egg with the cross got a chocolate rabbit.

In spite of the light-hearted chatter and the warm, sunny day, I felt forlorn and I couldn't explain it except to say I felt left out of Joanne's life nowadays.

I looked at Joanne and said, "I think we'd better get a divorce. You don't need me any more."

"Honey, I know what's wrong. If you would put Jesus first and me second and the kids third, everything would be okay. Why don't you come to a Bible study with me? Why don't you talk to Merlyn about it?"

"Joanne, I can't talk to Merlyn because she's part of the problem. She's like a rival. You're spending more time with her than with me."

Joanne shook her head no.

"I'm spending more time with God, Rudy. He's your rival. Merlyn only listens to me. You know, it's really funny. I call her up and tell her these fantastic things I'm finding in the Bible like I'm the first one ever to discover them. She doesn't say, 'Joanne, everybody knows that.' She just listens and explains gently what it all means and I'm learning so much! I'm like a hungry child who can't get enough food to satisfy him. I'm just starved to hear all these wonderful things I never knew were in the Bible before."

Something she said struck me as very real and I was touched. About a week later I went to a prayer meeting at a chapel not far from where we lived. I listened to the men praying and I thought, what have I got myself into? I can't stand up and pray out loud when it's my turn!

God spoke to my heart and let me know that I'd never really put Jesus first in my life. He'd been patient long

New Life

enough. Now it was time to step out and make a choice.

I closed my eyes and didn't actually realize I was speaking. I just gave my heart to Jesus. Then I began to cry. The men accepted me in a warm and friendly manner. God touched me in a special way that night and after that everything was different. Now I understood how Joanne felt and we were able to share everything in common again.

One by one the Lord is touching all our children. We don't have to make them go to church; they often wake us up on Sunday because they want to go.

I understand that changes are going on in all denominations now—Baptist, Catholic, Methodist and others—but in 1974 it was still fairly uncommon to see groups of people of all faiths coming together for prayer. At the convent where Joanne had lived for four years change has also taken place and now it has actually become a center for religious renewal. When Joanne was there in the fifties it was less open.

"Those were the static years. Changes came soon after," Sister Marguerite Frances Goodwin said of that time.

I couldn't get over the feeling that God was changing our lives inside and out, completing what He had begun that Christmas Eve in 1971 when He sent Mary Margaret to our house in Cedar Knolls. I knew it was all for the better. I knew also that we would have to trust Him.

Actually, we have always trusted God to comfort us where the children are concerned, since so many come and go even when we've become attached to them. Two young girls, ages ten and eleven, who were living in our home as foster children were taken back by their mother. We would have loved to have adopted these sisters, but the mother wanted them back and they had to go.

There were several other brothers and sisters in the same family. The house caught fire one day and our two little girls and five of their brothers and sisters died.

We were really broken up over this because we had grown to love these little girls as our own two daughters. It was quite awhile before we really felt at ease when the agencies sent us more foster children. Joanne was sad and hurt but she said to me, "Rudy, we can't let this stop us from loving the children who need love. We know that's the risk we take every time a new child comes into our home. These are God's children and He'll take care of the heartaches. It's worth the risk."

8

The House Full of Children

It was early spring, in April or May, 1975, after Joanne and I had experienced a life-changing spiritual renewal, that Joanne was looking through the Sunday paper and saw a picture of a large house for sale in Peapack, New Jersey.

She came running to find me.

"Oh, Rudy, look at this house. It would be just perfect for us! Nineteen rooms and seven baths—wouldn't that be great?"

I thought, oh, here she goes again! She used to do these crazy things but I had to admit they usually worked out. I hardly gave this a second thought though. Nineteen rooms? We'd never be able to afford a place like that.

I hadn't reckoned on a woman who only needed a challenge to have things start happening. The first thing I knew she had cut the picture of this huge house out of the paper and pasted it on the refrigerator door.

She started telling everybody that God was going to move us into that house someday. She was very convincing because I began to believe it too. I found out later there's a biblical principle involved here. "Truly I say to you, whoever says to this mountain, 'Be taken up and cast into the sea,' and does not doubt in his heart, but believes what he says is going to happen; it shall be granted him" (Mark 11:23).

"Thus says the Lord of hosts, the God of Israel, as follows: 'As for you and your wives, you have spoken with your mouths and fulfilled it with your hands' " (Jer. 44:25).

In other words, Joanne believed that God would bring this to pass and every time she said it was going to happen, her faith grew stronger that it would happen. I'd like to report that mine was just as strong, but it wasn't. Still, if that was the Lord's plan I was certainly willing.

One Saturday afternoon I told Joanne, "Get your coat and the kids and we'll go look at your house."

She was tickled to death and ran around gathering up children and piling them into the car. Everybody was excited. I tried to calm them down by saying, "Now don't get your hopes up. This thing may well be out of our reach. We're just going to have a look at it. No harm in that."

The real estate agent took us all through the house and I had to admit it was pretty impressive on the inside. The price was impressive also, one hundred, fifteen thousand dollars. We told the agent we liked it but didn't have a penny. He thought I was a minister who needed it for a school or an orphanage, after seeing all the children.

We told him no, this was just our own family. We needed a bigger place to live and we felt God wanted us to move into this very house. He didn't act shocked, didn't throw us out of his office, so we told him we'd be back.

The House Full of Children

Then we really began to pray in earnest. We received such an abundance of faith that the house would be ours. Joanne took the picture of the house with her to work at the hospital, telling everyone about it.

People told us, "You can never buy that house. How are you going to carry the mortgage? You won't be able to do it."

We went back to see the real estate agent. "Make me an offer," he said.

While we'd been praying about the house, the figure of ninety thousand dollars came to us, so that's what we offered him. He looked astonished, then threw up his hands and shook his head.

"Well, let's make them this offer," he said dubiously. "Let's see what they say."

Initially the owners said "No!"

With a feeling of resignation I sighed, "I guess we're not supposed to have that house."

A week later I got a phone call saying, "The house is yours!"

Now we had a house in Chester, New Jersey, and a ninety-thousand-dollar house in Peapack. Ordinarily a thing like that would have made me panic but this time it didn't. We went ahead with our plans and began to have peace.

Just before the closing of the house I had to call the owner and say, "I'm shy two thousand dollars for the closing payment. I'm sorry; I guess the deal is off."

"Never mind," said the owner. "I'll lend it to you, but this is the last time!"

He did. At the closing the banker wanted to know what

I did for a living and what kind of salary I made. We had to laugh, for it was definitely not enough of an income to take care of this house.

We found we had to take a double mortgage on the new house, plus the one we had on the Chester house and there we were holding three mortgages. Impossible! Nevertheless, we moved into our new home in August, 1975, complete with the down payment and everything in order. The Chester house was rented at first and then sold in December, so we were able to pay back the loans.

It was really something the day we moved into what was once an old mansion in Peapack called Maple Cottage, the historic Kate Macy Ladd home. It was located on four-and-a-half acres of land, three stories of house to fill with our six rooms of furniture.

The house itself was really grand-looking inside. When we walked through the front door from one of the three porches, the first thing we saw was a huge foyer with a wide staircase leading to the upstairs rooms, branching off to the left and the right at the second level.

Joanne said, "Honey, doesn't this remind you of something from the movies?"

She ran around, overseeing where all the furniture would go. We had only one couch for a living room that would easily hold four of them. She designated where this child and that child would sleep. We had a total of ten children then and they lost no time exploring every nook and cranny of every room and closet. They played outside on an old rope swing which hung from one of the tall, old trees. Then they climbed the trees or hurried off to explore the barn and stable.

The House Full of Children

The first meal we prepared and ate in the new house gave me indigestion, for I'd suddenly developed a bad case of "buyer's fright." How could we have been so bold as to purchase a house this size, carrying a mortgage payment of nine hundred and eleven dollars a month, on the salary I made as building and grounds supervisor for the Morristown school system? I knew God meant for us to trust Him but He surely didn't mean for us to be foolhardy. Why couldn't we have trusted Him and stayed in the Chester house?

I had to admit it had been too small for our needs and we were convinced that we were supposed to take in children who were sent to us.

Then God let me see that this was truly His house and He would provide for us.

"You are to take in anyone who comes or is brought to the door and I will provide."

As plain as day I felt that message get through to me. I shared this with Joanne.

She just smiled. "Oh, Rudy, of course He'll provide for us if we try to do what He wants us to do. He'll look out for us, you wait and see."

Before we moved to Peapack I had started praying that I might find a job that would pay more money. Then I kind of forgot about it in the shock of moving in and getting settled. God hadn't forgotten. Shortly after we moved I got a call from the school district of Mountain Lakes, a community not too far from us. They wanted me to apply for a position they had open for supervisor of grounds and buildings.

I applied, went over and took a look around. I knew

right away this was where I was supposed to be. I said I'd take the job. There was a big increase in pay and I had my first lesson in how God would provide. I hated to leave the people I'd worked with for eighteen years, for they were very kind to me. I knew so many of the students personally. It was an unexpected pleasure when they put in their yearbook that my leaving was Morristown's loss. It was my loss too.

Shortly thereafter, Joanne had a nudge from God to make a change in her life also. For seventeen years she had worked at various hospitals: St. Mary's, St. Claire's, All Souls, St. Anne's Villa, an old sisters' home, and for the past eighteen months at Lyons Veterans Hospital.

We had never had any difficulty between us about managing the children. I worked daytimes, she worked evenings and the kids helped each other and themselves. Drawing on our navy and convent backgrounds, we had instituted a strict atmosphere of discipline and mutual help, so we really never had a major problem on that score.

The older children made out the weekly schedules and everybody had a job to do. If somebody fell down on his job then the next week he had to be in charge of making out the schedule and seeing that it was carried out. The older girls helped with teeth brushing for the younger school children and with diapering and washing the babies. Certain ones made the lunches, some made the beds and helped with the breakfast dishes. Everything got done and no one person felt overburdened. It's been my theory right along that kids need and welcome responsibility although they may give you a hard time

The House Full of Children

about it at first. Nobody can have much self-respect if he never contributes anything worthwhile to life.

Now back to the lady of the house, our nurse in residence. I was completely surprised when she told me what she felt God had instructed her to do one Sunday while we were in church. She nudged me with her elbow and whispered, "Rudy, I feel God telling me I should quit my job and stay home full time."

"What!"

I almost fell off the pew in surprise. I looked at her very carefully to make sure she was feeling okay.

In the car going home I asked, "What was this you were telling me about quitting your job?"

"That was it, Rudy. I felt God asking me, *Who do you trust, Joanne, yourself or me?* I realized I had trusted myself for thirty-seven years and now I needed to trust Him.

"It'll be all right, Rudy. If we really trust Him then He'll take care of all our needs because He said whoever He sends to us, we should take and He would provide for them."

I had to admit it scared me at first, the prospect of losing her paycheck. She told the baby-sitter she wouldn't need her any more, then she gave her notice at Lyons Hospital.

Her supervisor was very upset, and tried to talk Joanne into taking a few days off instead but Joanne said no. She agreed to work two weeks longer and then she'd stay home.

She told me how she prayed all the way home, wanting God to let her know she'd done the right thing. She had gone to work that last day to submit her resignation, keeping Mary Frances home from school to look after the little ones. As soon as she got in the door, Mary Frances handed her a telephone message. Joanne was to call a certain number.

It was the children's bureau wanting to know if we could take three little children who had been abused. The woman began to tell her about the children.

"Oh, you don't have to tell me about them. Just bring them over. We'll take them."

She didn't have to question, for she knew it was God's way of telling her she was doing right. Sometimes we laugh when she starts to wonder if she should go back to work, for whenever we consider this we immediately get another child.

"I think the answer is no, Joanne," I told her. "Forget about it."

From that day on we began to lean more heavily on God for support, trusting Him to supply what we lacked. Children started to come from all different sources; help came too, in most unusual ways.

I remember one noontime we were at the big table with kids lined up all around. Joanne had mentioned that we didn't have money for food for the rest of the week. I didn't have a dime in my pocket. Several big expenses were looming up and I was feeling discouraged. It was sixteen-year-old Rudy, Jr.'s turn to say grace and this is what he said.

"God, we thank you for this food. You promised to provide for us and we need help. Thank you, God."

I had such a lump in my throat I could hardly swallow.

The House Full of Children

As soon as the dishes were cleared and washed I made some sort of excuse to go out. I remembered I hadn't been to the post office so I drove to town, mainly for an excuse to get out of the house.

I stopped at the post office and collected a few more bills and a white envelope from a church we'd been attending. I scattered them on the table when I got back home, not really having much desire to open them.

Joanne picked them up and said, "Here's a letter from Long Hill Chapel. Why didn't you open it, Rudy?"

She opened it and a check for fifty dollars fell out. We just stood and looked at each other with our mouths open in amazement. Then we showed it to Rudy, Jr. He needed to know how God had answered his prayer. We knew then that God was faithful.

As more children came, questions came also, from people who said, "How is this affecting your own children when you take in so many outsiders? It's not fair to them, is it?"

Joanne and I really pondered and prayed over this. Was it unfair to our biological children to ask them to share their home, their parents, their belongings with other children who had nothing?

Joanne made this comparison one day: "I wonder how many people said to Abraham, 'Hey, that's a great thing you're doing for Isaac, sacrificing him on the mountain.'

"Maybe they're saying, 'Hey, Joanne and Rudy, that's a great thing you're doing for Rudy, Mary Ann, Mary Frances, Robert, Matthew and Mary Claire by taking in all those other children.'

"Are we sacrificing our own kids? Are we being unfair

to ask them to share their home and our love with so many others?"

Then she went on to talk about Noah and how people didn't understand what he was doing.

"What did people think when they saw him building that big boat? They didn't understand, did they? They probably said, 'Noah, you know it hardly ever rains here. Are you crazy?'"

I got the picture but I didn't have the answer, that is, not until I'd met Jesus in a personal way in 1975. Then our children met Him. That cleared up a lot of things for us. We are all God's children, all in His family. It seems only natural that one should help another. That's what we believe. That's the way we live, all of us. I don't say it's been perfect. Lots of times the kids have had trouble adjusting to one another, but we feel they're one family.

When people ask me now which ones are mine I just say, "They're all mine." The children have come to realize that it doesn't take away from them when we invite other little ones in. It's more like it multiplies our love and our feelings of being a family.

The older ones enjoy playing with the little ones and cuddling them. It's amazing how little love and cuddling some children get and how much they all need.

When little Timmy came to us the next year, he had been kept in a hospital with all white walls and furnishings for the first three months of his life. For the longest time this little tyke was petrified of anything with color. Bright colors of red, green and yellow would make him panic.

Gradually he has lost his fear of color and noise. He plays with a small, red, stuffed dog and jiggles the play-gym on his playpen. At fifteen months, Timmy watches television and sings along with it. Or he'll just sing when there's nobody around but him.

Changes like this impress all the children and make them glad to be a part of God's work.

Some of the mistreated and mistrustful ones take longer to change. Some change right away. Others don't respond for a long time but we go on loving them and helping them. Only God can give us that kind of love.

I remember one summer when Joanne was pregnant with Matthew, before we moved into the Peapack house, we had taken all the children to the Bronx Zoo for a Sunday outing. It was a very warm day and Joanne and I were worn out with watching the kids dart here and there, eager to see everything that was to be seen. We needed ten hands apiece. Robert wanted to see the penguins, Mary Frances wanted to see the exotic birds and they each had one of the little children by the hand.

Mary Ann and Rudy were buying snowcones for everybody at one of the stands and it was hard to keep an eye on everybody at once.

Suddenly Joanne said to me, "I've got to sit down. I'm getting weak all over."

Sure enough, her face was pale and her dark eyes looked enormous. I thought she was going to faint. We found a bench and she sat down; beginning to moan, she loosened her collar and breathed heavily.

The man and woman sitting beside her got up and hurried off, fearing probably that she was drunk or on drugs. I tried to massage her wrists and looked around for Rudy to send him for water. Joanne was looking worse by the minute.

"Rudy, I don't think I'm going to make it. I can't get my breath. I think I'm dying," she whispered to me.

You see, at that point I didn't have the peace of the Lord that I received two years later and I became angry. I jumped up and yelled: "Joanne, don't die on me like this and leave me with all these kids!"

All I could think of was myself. What would happen to me if she died and left the whole flock in my care? I didn't have to find out, for she recovered shortly, after a rest and a cold drink.

Our attitudes have had to change along with those of the children. Sometimes it's the natural instinct of a parent to react with anger to a hostile child. That's the human way, but God gives an inner conviction of His peace that makes it easier to react in love. He gives us understanding of the children by His Word such as is written in Matthew 18.

Jesus once called a little child to Him and stood the child in the midst of the disciples: "Truly I say to you, unless you are converted and become like children, you shall not enter the kingdom of heaven. Whoever then humbles himself as this child, he is the greatest in the kingdom of heaven. And whoever receives one such child in my name receives me" (Matt. 18:3-5).

God has put us in a position of having to trust Him for all our needs. We've had to look to Him in childlike faith and it has certainly made us more understanding of children. Which is probably what He had in mind all along.

People want to know where the children come from and

how we can afford to adopt them. They come from the state and county bureaus or from Spaulding for Children, a private, nonprofit New Jersey agency. A Catholic agency has also sent us a child. Some have come in the middle of the night; some we are called to go and get.

The very first adoption cost us three hundred fifty dollars; the second one cost one hundred fifty. Now we can adopt without charge for we have a wonderful Jewish lawyer who requires no fees for adoption of children not subsidized by the state. He knows our faith is strong and he once asked us to pray for his own son. The social workers don't understand the source of our strength and one remarked to Joanne that she couldn't send us any more children, because we had too many already. She did soon after though. Their attitudes are changing too.

It is most rewarding when we see changes occur in the foster children, some of whom we are able to adopt and some we are not. One young man, fifteen, and his thirteen-year-old sister were sent to us for help. The girl went back to her mother in a couple of weeks but the boy stayed on and was sent to school. He was in the eighth grade but was reading on a third-grade level. His teacher was questioning him, trying to draw out his capabilities, but he always had an excuse.

"I'm a nonreader. I'm perceptually impaired."

Fortunately the teacher didn't take his word for it and in time he made good progress. There were some things he could do better than the best readers in his class. He liked to sell things. When the class sold candy for a project, he sold more than anyone else and kept track of the money perfectly.

OUR GROWING FAMILY

We lost this young fellow. His mother wanted him back. We don't know where he is now but he knows that he can always come back if he wants to. Our door is always open.

One of the major problems we had when we moved to Peapack was getting the children into the right schools and the right classes. I think I'll save that for Joanne to tell since she spent so much time conferring with teachers, reading specialists and principals. I just want to tell about an incident when Robert was in seventh grade and had to do a report on Greek history.

As was my custom since we'd moved into the bigger house, I gathered the kids around the long table in the dining room for their evening Bible study. The little ones, Mary Claire, three, Mary Christine, Matthew and Frankie, each four, had gone upstairs with Joanne to get ready for bed.

I read to them from Psalm 107. I didn't dream of how far I was going to digress before we got through with that psalm. I had intended to dwell on the early verses about God delivering the people who had wandered in the wilderness regions in hunger and thirst. I wanted to stress how He had led them out of their distresses, providing bountifully for them, for I saw this as a clear picture of how God was providing for our own needs.

I hadn't read far when Mary Ann asked me to back up to verses twenty-three and twenty-four. I read again those verses.

Those who go down to the sea in ships,
Who do business in great waters;

The House Full of Children

They have seen the works of the Lord,
And His wonders in the deep.

After I'd read it she said something that surprised me. "Daddy, you've never kept your promise to tell me how it was when you were on a destroyer sailing around on the ocean. Remember you said you would some day?"

I had promised her that when she was about eleven years old and here she was almost fifteen. How could she have remembered that long-ago conversation we'd had beside the swimming pool on our trip to Colorado?

Robert, twelve, chimed in. "Daddy, tell us about Greece. I have to make a report on some of those old buildings, you know, the Acropolis and some of the others."

The rest of the kids nodded and began to put in their two cents' worth. So I sent Mary Ann upstairs to get an old blue album out of the middle drawer of my decrepit desk and changed our Bible study from a present-day application of God's help to how He had directed my life when I was just a teen-ager, only a little older than Rudy was now.

After a short prayer for God to help me teach the children something out of all this, I opened the scrapbook which most of them had seen at one time or another. None of them really knew how God had been leading me by His compass as far back as 1950.

First they had to see the pictures of old dad playing basketball in Clifton, New Jersey, when I was a boy. I have lots of yellowed clippings and pictures of me playing center or guard for the Clifton Sokols, the Clifton Vets or St. Francis High School.

"Were you pretty good in basketball, dad?" Robert asked.

"Not too bad, I guess. We played in all the local tournaments and in a couple of national tournaments.

"Yes, I was always pretty good at sports and once received a first-place award for track in the mile relay."

Mary Ann, blue-eyed, blonde, and the athlete in the family, wondered if I'd ever considered making sports a career.

"No, Mary Ann, I never seriously considered that. Fact is, I didn't have my heart set on any particular career until I started a part-time job in a bakery, washing pots and pans. Then I got the desire to learn how to bake, so I learned right from scratch.

"Soon it wasn't enough to be doing it part time. I decided to quit school and work at it full time. I quit in my senior year and began to be a baker."

I saw Rudy, sixteen, give me a funny look and I remembered we'd just talked the week before about a friend of his who had dropped out of school. I had given him a stern lecture on the benefits of staying in school and learning.

I jumped ahead of my story, striking while the iron was hot.

"No, I didn't graduate with my class but I was a very lucky guy, for I was able to get my diploma later while on board the destroyer. I not only studied for that, I took the college entrance exams and got accepted at Oklahoma A. and M. College in Stillwater, Oklahoma."

Out of the corner of my eye I saw Rudy relax and exhale a sigh of relief. Now he could believe what his old man told

The House Full of Children

him about the value of education. He couldn't have, if I had said one thing and done another.

Mary Frances, fourteen, spoke up. "Daddy, finish the story. When did you join the navy?"

"It was sometime in 1950 that I decided to join up, during the Korean conflict. They sent me to the Great Lakes, the world's largest naval training center."

One of the younger boys wanted to know if it was boot camp. He'd probably heard about that in some old movie on TV.

"Yeah, that was boot camp or basic training. Whatever you called it, it meant for sure that we learned how to be neat, orderly and on time."

I showed them some pictures of how we had to roll our clothes and lay them out in apple-pie order for inspection. We grumbled about the discipline and about having to scrub the barracks floors twice a day but just the same we felt a sense of pride when the place looked spotless.

"Like us, daddy," Eric, seven, spoke up. "Like you make us clean our rooms."

"That's right, Eric. Just like that."

"But when did you get to sea?" Mary Frances wanted to know.

"I'm coming to that, honey. We had about eight weeks of basic training, then I got my first two-day leave and came home to Jersey to see mom and dad. That was Christmas, 1950."

Mary Ann wondered if Aunt Helen, Uncle Johnny and Uncle Joe were there too.

"They were there, Mary Ann, but not quite like you know them today. Aunt Helen was a nurse and living at home. Uncle Johnny was grown up and working. Your Uncle Joe was just three years old. He was the kid brother."

"You didn't have as many brothers and sisters as we do, did you?" It was Michael, nine, who spoke up.

I told him no.

The kids were passing around the pictures from the album, some I'd taken in Chicago when a couple of my good buddies and I had gone sightseeing. I always had my camera along, taking pictures of snowy Lincoln Park or Lake Michigan. There were some pictures of mom, Helen, little Joe and me in New York City where we had gone to see the Christmas window at Macy's and all the decorations.

"I hated to say good-by to the folks that Christmas because I knew I'd be shipped out in a few weeks. I didn't know where I'd go. I expected to be sent on active duty with my outfit but it didn't happen that way. The whole company but me was assigned to the *USS New Jersey*, and I was sent to a destroyer that was still in dry dock in Charleston, South Carolina."

Mary Elizabeth, eleven, asked, "What's dry dock?"

"Dry dock? Well, that's where ships go to get worked over and fixed up so they can go to sea. In that kind of dock the water can be pumped out so the ships can be repaired easier.

"This destroyer, the *Stoddard*, was about to be recommissioned so there was only a skeleton crew aboard. A few reserves, a few boots—"

"Daddy, you don't mean real skeletons and real boots, do you?" Mary Elizabeth asked.

The House Full of Children

Rudy, Jr., who suddenly became a sixteen-year-old authority, told her what I'd meant.

"Dad means a few sailors from boot camp and a few men from the naval reserves—a small crew, not skeletons. Right, dad?"

"Right, son."

I passed around a few more pictures, showing me doing mess cooking at Great Lakes and told them how I'd expected to be a baker on the *Stoddard* but instead they had made me a torpedo man.

"Finally I spoke up and told the chief that I'd been trained to be a baker and that's what I wanted to do.

"Well, there's only one baker on a ship and somebody was already doing the job, but they let me take a test anyway. I had to make and prepare a full menu. It was easy. I got the job."

Rudy held up the large, glossy picture I have of the *Stoddard* (DD 566), and asked what the numbers meant and how it got its name. I explained that destroyers are named for naval heroes and that *Stoddard* was named for a Civil War hero, James Stoddard.

"Different classes of ships have different sets of numbers. Now it's a funny thing about that number 566. See the big, white numerals painted on the gray bow of the ship? Well, I used to live at number 56 Cheever Avenue in Clifton. My company number was 256 and my serial number was 7195656. I felt that was where I was supposed to be, not just a funny coincidence. *Stoddard* was home to me for three years and nine months."

I hadn't realized that time was going by so fast. Joanne came downstairs to shoo seven-year-old Margy and Eric off to bed and the older ones off to do their homework. It was eight-thirty and I hadn't even gotten out of dry dock. The kids begged to stay and I would probably have agreed to finish off the story, at least I'd have gotten them as far as Greece, but Joanne insisted that we call it quits and let the kids get their homework done.

I helped one or two of them with spelling words and tucked in several with a hug and a prayer. I never did get to finish the lesson on "those who go down to the sea in ships." After the children were all in bed and Joanne was folding clothes, I made myself a cup of coffee and sat down again at the long table, piling pictures and souvenirs on the bench beside me so I could spread out the brown logbook from the *Stoddard*. It was a memory book in every sense of the word and what memories it brought back.

Rudy presides at a typical Sunday afternoon gathering of family and visiting friends.

A relaxing time of fellowship.

Joanne holds their youngest, Samuel.

Mary Frances, Robert, Mary Elizabeth

Mary Ann returns a fast serve.

Just posing. Mary Margaret, Mary Christine, a friend, Matthew, a friend, David and Frankie.

Jon and Samuel share a happy secret!

(Left) Doreen holds Mary Margaret while Mary Elizabeth watches the other children at play. (Right) Shaun Michael—attends school in North Dakota.

(Left) Happy smiles—Marty and Mary Christine (Right) Big sister Mary Grace with Mary Claire and Jon.

"Hooping it up." Bob, Robert, Mary Claire and a couple of guests.

Easy riders—Matthew, Mary Christine and Frankie.

Eric and Marty—two special boys.

Gasoline shortage? No problem here.

Maple Cottage—A house full of children and love.

9

Cook's Tour

I didn't see any live action during the Korean conflict. Everything going into action went out from the West Coast and they had sent me to the East Coast.

I boarded *Stoddard* in January, 1951, and from our home base in Boston we made several trial runs up and down the coast. That first summer we toured the Caribbean.

There, I had my first glimpse of the carefree life style of the people in Haiti, Jamaica and Puerto Rico. The weather was hot and people wore loose-fitting clothing, went barefoot, and wore big straw hats. I had pictures of little children wearing almost nothing at all, and of the women carrying huge baskets on top of their heads.

We spent a little time in Cuba at Guantanamo Bay, America's forty-five-square-mile naval base on the southern coast. "Gitmo," as it's called by everyone, was popular with the crew because of its good supply of American beer.

My favorite cruise was during the summer of 1953 when we joined the Sixth Fleet for exercises in the

OUR GROWING FAMILY

Mediterranean. We were to rendezvous with other ships of the flotilla, including the aircraft carrier, *Coral Sea*, a heavy cruiser and four destroyers.

The destroyers are really the suicide ships, expendable if need be. Somebody compared them to the cavalry of early days and to the tanks of today's army. They are there to make sure the aircraft carrier gets through.

Even with fleet exercises and maneuvers, our cruise was more of a good-will tour than work.

I looked at the logbook entry for April 18, 1953. It read like this:

0530 "Reveille! Reveille! Up all hands! Heave out and trice up!"

I could almost hear again the shrill scream of the boatswain's whistle that wakened us earlier than usual. Everyone was excited and rushing around, listening to the orders from the squawk box.

0545 "Now go to your stations all the Special Sea Detail. All hands fall in at quarters for leaving port."

Every one of us who could hurried topside to get a last look at the States, because we'd be gone for six months. The Officer of the Day shifted his watch to the bridge. The men on the buoy pulled the pin from the big shackle, watched as the chain slid into the water, then climbed into the waiting whaleboat to board the destroyer.

Main Control reported to the bridge that they were standing by to answer all bells. The deck force on the forecastle and the ordnance gang on the fantail were ordered to single up all lines.

0612 "Shift Colors!"

Stoddard backed slowly away from the two destroyers

Cook's Tour

moored alongside her and headed down the bay.

The first couple of days out we ran into some rough weather but it soon calmed down and began to get warmer. We passed Gibraltar on May 4, heading for Athens, Greece.

For the next six months we called at every port in southern Europe from Gibraltar to Split, Yugoslavia. It was like a living history lesson, which I'd always liked anyway. I saw sights I had never expected to see in my life. The Acropolis in May, all lit up at night, was a sight to behold.

I laid aside the pictures I'd made of the Acropolis and the tiny fragment of stone from its ruins, so that Robert could take them to his class to show when he did his report on Greece.

I didn't know what kind of mark Robert might get on his report but I was having a grade A trip looking through the hundreds of pictures and reading again the notes describing our tour.

We had sailed around the southern end of Greece, arriving in Salonika. Then we steamed through the Dardanelles and into Istanbul, right near Russia's back door. Just eight miles up the Bosporus was the Black Sea.

In Istanbul I had taken pictures of the Byzantine church of St. Sophia, built about A.D. 360, rebuilt in 532 and converted into a mosque in 1453. Many mornings we were awakened at three o'clock hearing the priests call the faithful to prayer.

From Istanbul we went back to Piraeus, Greece, for a few days, then sailed through the Strait of Messina to Golfe Juan, France. Two days later we were underway for

OUR GROWING FAMILY

our first fleet exercise, then we headed south for Tripoli, Libya. There we saw mosques, women in purdahs and several camels. My camera worked overtime.

When we'd come into port most of my buddies would hurry off to drink at the local bars, but I would grab my camera and start taking pictures.

It was a way of escaping the drinking and carousing most of the other guys wanted to do. I wanted to see the sights and enjoy a simpler way of life. Go with the crowd to the bar, or head for the nearest ice cream shop? I usually chose the ice cream.

The sailors teased me about that a lot and I didn't mind much. But one day I sort of boiled over and showed that I did mind.

I remember coming up on deck just as the boatswain's whistle sounded and *Stoddard* edged its way into crowded Valencia harbor. I was wondering whether or not I wanted to see a Spanish bullfight. Some of the men were going. I really had more interest in taking pictures of the famous bell towers of Valencia. *Stoddard* prepared for docking. It always fascinated me to see this long, gray mass slip gracefully into position, guided by unseen hands and by the orders that spewed out of the speakers. Then abruptly we had come around in place and the atmosphere was different. The whistle sounded again.

"Now hear this! Shore leave starts at thirteen hundred hours and ends at zero-six-hundred tomorrow. Seamen going ashore, pick up your gear and muster on the starboard side."

Looking toward the shore, it hardly seemed necessary to go into town, for it looked like the entire town had come

Cook's Tour

out to see us dock.

I had just stepped off the tender, wondering which way to go, when somebody slapped me on the back. I knew right away who it was when I heard the southern drawl. It was the rebel cook, Billy Bob Earl, the first person I'd ever met from "Etlanta," Georgia, and the only person I knew who had three first names, though one was his last.

Billy Bob hit me again on the back and I could feel my flesh tingle through the white cotton uniform.

"Well, if it ain't ol' shutterbug himself. Y'all comin' with us to soak up some of them larrupin' good rum drinks? Or are you goin' to the ice cream parlor instead?"

He turned to the other three mates and laughed. My shoulder still tingled.

Before I could answer Billy Bob slapped at my shoulder a third time.

"Come on, shutterbug. Pass up the ice cream today and see some high Spanish livin'. That sweet stuff'll rot your insides! Don't be a sissy, heah? Come on and have a drink."

I never did find my tongue. I didn't need to. I found my fist instead, hauled off and socked him on the chin. He hit the ground with a splat and the other fellows stood there open-mouthed.

He lay there a couple of minutes, got up, rubbing his jaw. I had no idea whether or not he'd lay one on me and bash my head in but I wasn't scared. It just seemed as if something told me this was the day I was supposed to stand up for myself and become a man instead of a shy, withdrawn, gangly kid.

Billy Bob looked at me in a different kind of way.

"Well, dang me, shutterbug, I didn't know you had it in you. Go on and get your ice cream. More power to you."

From that day on we became the best of friends. I taught him how to bake bread and cakes. Though I needed a good friend I wouldn't have set about getting one just that way. That's the way it happened though. It was a different kind of day for me, and I felt differently about myself after that. I guess you'd say I began to like myself better. I began to believe I was somebody.

When a pretty French girl invited me to visit her family on their yacht when we docked at Menton, France, my morale went a little higher still. She was a lovely girl and did her best to show me a good time. So did her mother, father, sister and brother.

While we were in Menton we celebrated the Fourth of July. Somebody decided it would be great if we gave a party for a group of French orphans. I was on liberty but they came looking for me so I could bake cookies and make ice cream for the kids. I don't know if the orphans understood why we were celebrating but they sure did go for the goodies.

That gave me a warm feeling, knowing the kids had enjoyed themselves. There was something about that crew of little folks, boys and girls, that touched my heart. They were clean, with combed hair. The girls wore colorful dresses and the boys had on clean, ironed shirts. Somebody loved those kids. They didn't fit exactly with my idea of an orphan—dirty, ragged, uncared for. I figured it must have been love that made the difference.

I had never baked for anybody before that gave me so much satisfaction. It was a little like I was giving them part of myself with the cakes, cookies and ice cream.

My reputation as a baker was getting around. I didn't use the regular navy recipes. I used the ones I'd learned from the bakery back home and from my mother's kitchen. The men really went for the hot, freshly-made breads, rolls and cakes. The navy did all the shopping for me but I had to requisition the things I needed. I soon became acquainted with big orders.

Once in a while we'd run out of certain things and it wasn't unusual to have the fellows trade with some of the carriers or other ships we docked alongside in port. They would trade so many pounds of potatoes for a certain kind of flour so I could bake something special. They loved to smell the fresh bread baking.

Because I baked at night I had time to think then and to meditate. I liked the quietness of the deck at midnight. That's when I spoke to God. Starting out I used to address Him as "God" but when we became more intimate, I remember just simply praying "Father."

"Father, I feel kind of lonesome tonight. We haven't had mail for a while and I'd really like to hear how my folks, Helen, Johnny and little Joe are doing.

"I wish there was someone I could talk to like this in person. None of the fellows seem to want to share this way. Oh, Tugboat comes in sometimes and talks about how life was in Brooklyn when he was a kid and how he helped his old man run the tugs. Billy Bob always wants to talk about girls. That kind of leaves me out. I don't know that much about girls.

"God, I wish I knew what you have in store for me when my hitch is up. What's my life going to be like? I guess what I'm asking for is a look over the horizon.

"Maybe I don't actually want to know, Father, what it is you've got cut out for me to do. I just want to do what you want me to do. For now it's enough to be in the middle of this big ocean, heading for Turkey. I leave it all up to you.

"Lord, thank you for listening to me. Guess I'll hit the sack now. Good night."

I don't remember that I ever ended a prayer with "amen." It seemed like every prayer always ended with "Good night" or "So long."

I don't know that I thought much about Jesus although I certainly acknowledged Him as my Savior but I was forever carrying on a conversation with God. Not out loud. If I'd done that the seamen would have thought I was slightly off my rocker. It was just a matter of talking to Him as I stirred up a batch of dough. Sometimes I'd be quiet and listen to the sounds that came from Him inside my heart. These silent times were the best for me.

By the end of my second year on the *Stoddard*, I had no secrets that I tried to keep from God. He knew everything about me. This gave me a real sense of peace I had never found anywhere else. I figured if He knew all the ins and outs of my life and still could put up with me, then life would have a way of working out. I decided to leave it all in His hands.

I began to feel at home on the *Stoddard* and made a few more friends. It wasn't long before I had the opportunity to continue my schooling, like I had told young Rudy, so I could get a high school diploma. I had quite a bit of time to study and read. History always had a strong appeal for me which is why I enjoyed calling at the exotic foreign ports.

I dug up all the information I could about the destroyer I was on. *Stoddard* was first commissioned in April, 1944, and saw service in World War II in the Kuril Islands and in Okinawa. She had been damaged by *Kamikaze* fire. *Stoddard* was present in Tokyo Bay for the signing of the truce with Japan and was decommissioned in January, 1946. I was proud to have had a part in her second sea career.

We rounded out our Mediterranean cruise with more fleet exercises and then up the Adriatic to the Free Territory of Trieste, city of American milk shakes, American hamburgers, American beer and American M.P.s! Boy, did we feel at home there.

One of the last ports we visited was Venice, the city with the streets of water. It's always been noted for being a playground of the rich and the week we were there it was loaded with movie stars. Some of the starlets came on board and we took their pictures. We learned that an international film festival was going on. Rex Harrison and Lili Palmer came aboard the night we showed their movie, *The Four Poster*. We found out later she had won the top actress award at the festival.

A few more exercises, a trip back to the Riviera, a big NATO exercise and we were soon to head back home. Besides commissary duty I'd had my share of other duty. When general quarters were sounded I had to take up my station in the depth charges area. It was my responsibility to pull the lanyard and release the charges. I was glad these were only practice runs and not the real thing though we never really knew when it might be for real.

OUR GROWING FAMILY

On the seventeenth of October, 1953, we refueled at Gibraltar and headed home. I had many pictures to show and many stories to tell my folks.

Dad was a good man, acquainted with God. He made us kids toe the line in his quiet way. He would wait outside for me when I was ready to catch the bus to go back to base and walk me down to the bus stop.

"Do you need any money?" he would ask.

If it was raining, he'd wait there with an umbrella, but he didn't want anybody to see him doing that. They might have thought him a softy, which he was at heart, but he tried not to show it. I admired him a lot.

I was on my second cruise to the Mediterranean when word came that my father had had a heart attack. I couldn't believe it. I didn't know whether or not I'd be able to go home or if I did whether he'd still be alive. I spoke to the captain about it. It was then that I found out how many friends I had on the *Stoddard*. Not only did I get leave to return home but my shipmates chipped in three hundred dollars of their own money to fly me back. I flew from Spain to Naples, to Algiers, to Port Lyautey, to the Azores, over the Pawtuxet River, then to Maryland and home.

God was good. Not only did I see my dad alive, but I saw him recover. He lived for ten years after that.

Back on the *Stoddard* I received a hero's welcome, the guys were so glad to get my baking again. I got caught up in my studying and decided to take a test for college, thinking that's what I would do when my hitch was up. I passed the test and applied for a scholarship to Oklahoma A. and M. College, expecting to enroll there in

Cook's Tour

September, 1954.

On June 25, 1954, I was mustered out of the navy and left the *Stoddard*. In a way I was sad about it and yet in another way I felt I was about to begin a new adventure. I would soon be twenty-one years old and was looking forward to college.

Closing the book on my seagoing memories of 1954, I came back to the present moment of 1976. Here I was in Peapack, New Jersey, the father of thirteen children, wondering how I'd gotten from there to here. Was this the plan God had for me when I'd decided to let Him take over my life back on shipboard those long years ago? I believe it is. I believe I'm right where I'm supposed to be at this very time.

The house was quiet because it was late now. I had supposed Joanne had long since gone to bed but she hadn't. She had been ironing and doing more laundry. There was always laundry that needed doing. She sat down on the bench beside me and picked up the blue picture book.

"Looking back over your past, huh? Is this the book with the pictures of the French girls from Cannes?"

"Yeah, but there are not as many as I remembered. They're not as pretty either."

Joanne laughed, and said she wanted to look through the album before I put it away.

"Robert wants some pictures for his report and Mary Ann wants to hear more about my sailing days. Just leave them on the table when you're finished."

10

Baker's Dozen

Living in a house with nineteen rooms and seven baths, big enough so that everybody was able to have a spot of his or her own, felt great! It was wonderful to be able to spread out thirteen children in bright, spacious rooms with drawers and closets for their belongings, toys, books and personal treasures. The older children had rooms of their own to decorate as they pleased. The younger ones doubled up.

It was thrilling to see the children playing in the big yard with four-plus acres to roam in, huge old maple trees to climb, a barn to explore, places for hiding. What a beautiful house our heavenly Father had supplied for our needs!

We were in the original Maple Cottage that was once part of the Kate Macy Ladd estate, which covered over four hundred acres along Peapack Road, spilling over into three or four communities. According to local history, our house was once a convalescent center for working women who needed rest and care on a short-term basis. Due to Mrs. Ladd's generosity, this was provided free.

OUR GROWING FAMILY

The convalescent center is now housed in the three-story mansion that was the Ladd residence in Far Hills, New Jersey. Kate Macy Ladd, heiress and philanthropist, if alive, would probably be happy to see the children playing in the yard and climbing her big, old maple trees. The house is full of children, laughter and a few tears. Now it has sufficient furniture too. In the beginning we rattled around in many unfurnished rooms.

Besides the bedrooms we had two big dining rooms, a den, library and a forty-foot living room to furnish. It was about three months after we moved in that God started supplying our needs for furniture. The first exciting experience was when one of the elders at Long Hill Chapel told us to go to the Market Street Mission and pick out several pieces of furniture. Rudy and I took Matthew with us and he saw a big, red fire truck and the Lord even gave him that. In the months that followed, furniture came from many different sources. Amazingly enough, it always came before we actually needed it. It seemed to almost take on a pattern; whenever more furniture came, we could expect more children.

Soon our home was comfortably and neatly furnished. The big, sunny living room with its two enormous windows now has three couches and lovely curtains at the windows.

During a part of this time of getting settled in our new home I didn't even have money for gas. I knew God had a purpose in my not being able to go anywhere even if I couldn't see it at the time. One day I noticed an advertisement for calligraphy in the *Daily Record*. The ad demonstrated how calligraphy looks; they had used the

Baker's Dozen

Scripture reference: "Let your light so shine before men that they may see your good works, and glorify your Father which is in heaven" (Matt. 5:16 KJV). We had this huge wall in the dining room and nothing to decorate it with, so I carefully painted the words on the wall, in calligraphy.

It was not long afterward that we realized this was the perfect verse for our family.

One day I decided that the rather small kitchen needed remodeling. I covered part of the walls with cedar shakes which not only looked and smelled nice but gave me a ready-made bulletin board for attaching pictures of the children, notes for everybody and many other items.

The wide staircase, with its white pillars and shiny bannisters that lead from the center hall to the second floor, has been a source of enjoyment for us. Sometimes I like to stand and look up the stairs at the window directly above them when the morning sun shines through. If I climb the stairs, I know I can look out and see the side yard where our much prayed for pool sits. Our good friend Raymond not only gave us the pool but it would not be standing if it were not for his help in putting it up.

I even enjoyed the nice laundry room where I sometimes did five or six loads of laundry a day. Between loads I could be found usually listening to a tape, reading a book or studying the Bible. I began to be able to get out occasionally for women's luncheons and fellowship gatherings, sometimes being asked to speak at one or the other or at a church meeting. I had worked for seventeen years in hospitals because I enjoyed people. I needed to give to people but I also needed to receive something for myself.

Then we had a great idea, and we realized it was from God, supplying another need we hadn't as yet prayed about. Rudy and I felt we shouldn't go out together in the evening and leave all the children so we decided to pray about someone starting a Bible study in our own home. He had already been teaching the children, but Rudy didn't feel qualified to teach adults.

A year later, a beautiful man from our church offered to teach a class in our home. Word got around and soon people were coming from all over. What a gathering it was. Rudy walked into the living room one Thursday night and saw a beautiful new lamp on the table. He asked, "Where did that lamp come from?"

One of the men spoke up. "I brought it. I like to have lots of light when I read."

So that's how our living room received more light. God began to shed His light on the Scriptures for us and all who came. That light was warm, loving and caring. It shone on the little ones around us and melted away all our reserve. So we were ready to welcome nine-year-old David when he was sent to us for help.

He was a thin, little fellow, lonely looking, with a short, blond crew cut. He had several problems. He had to wear a prosthesis to replace an eye he had lost in an accident. He had lived in foster homes for several years. At our house he discovered he wasn't the only one with impaired vision. Our Mary Elizabeth had also lost an eye accidentally as a young child.

Our son Robert was born with congenital blindness in one eye. Robert knows about pain and waiting for six operations to restore his bilateral cleft lip and palate. He knows God can restore and heal and give life, love and joy. He is in fact a great joy-spreader, the family "ham," always acting, wanting everyone to have a good time.

David's reading teacher worked miracles in his life. When she first became acquainted with him he appeared nervous, hyperactive, and supposedly had a low IQ. He couldn't remember anything for any length of time—"low auditory memory," I think they called it.

The principal at his school wanted him to be sent to another school because he thought David couldn't keep up with the other children. This dedicated young teacher looked beyond the child's faults and imperfections and saw his possibilities. She taught him ten or twelve Bible verses, helped him add and multiply, think and reason. Then she took him to the principal and said, "See! David has something to show you."

David proved his ability and remained in that school until recently when he was transferred to a special school in Mendham.

He's had to prove his stamina in lots of ways. Being rather slight for his age and always thin, he found that the larger boys would pick on him. One afternoon I was called by the school nurse and told to come and get him. He'd been involved in an accident. Some of the students were pushing and teasing him and he got shoved down on the ground, hitting his good eye on a piece of wood.

I sent Rudy, Jr. to pick him up at school and he came in sobbing. I was sitting in the dining room peeling what seemed to be hundreds of potatoes someone had given us.

I put my arm around him and asked him to tell me what

had happened. His eye was red but it didn't look damaged.

"We prayed for your eye, David."

He sobbed a little more then said, "It feels better."

"God did it, David. He healed your eye. What do you think you ought to do now?"

"I have to forgive the boys who did it."

"That's right, honey. You have to forgive them."

I'll never forget the look that came across his face. It was his old rebellious look, but not quite. He looked down at his sneaker, and when he looked up at me it was as if a burden had been lifted off his shoulders. His face was innocent-looking again.

"I forgive them, mom."

David was free again. By forgiving his enemies he didn't have to carry around a burden of hatred and resentment. I gave him a kiss and sent him to wash his face and hands. His tears were all gone, his eye was all right and David had learned a big lesson.

He still has a problem of slowing down when he gets too active. He doesn't know when to stop but he hasn't had to take medication for over a year. Best of all, he's beginning to feel he belongs with us. Until now he had never accepted a foster parent's name but he tells us he wants to be called Sheptock.

His insecurity increases when he's been allowed to return to his natural parents for a visit. His teacher tells me she always knows when a foster child has been in contact with the natural parent.

"The child seems to have difficulty for days after," she says.

Such struggles and heartaches between human beings

can only cause difficulty. Only the grace of God can alleviate such problems. And that's why we look to Him.

The first year we lived in Peapack I was always running back and forth to school, conferring with the teachers, the principal or the nurse.

One day I asked one of the teachers why Mary Elizabeth was having such a difficult time in fifth grade.

We sat in her small office in the school which has maybe two hundred students, kindergarten through eighth grade. This teacher very seriously explained what had happened since we moved into the community and had enrolled our children in public school.

"This is a very small community and some children have difficulties accepting some of the new students. You're 'new' if you've been here five years. Mary Elizabeth is very new and interracial. She is pretty, but extremely quiet. She has a problem communicating verbally. I don't think she was ever talked to much in her early years. All that serves to make her different and difference is something not to be easily accepted by her peers."

The teacher then assured me that most of our children were advancing well with some help.

"In fact," she continued, "this school system owes your family a vote of thanks. Not only has it taught us to adjust to different types of children but it has been instrumental in our establishing the first child-study team for the district. What a blessing that's been for kids and teachers alike. Now we can deal with the children who come in and say, 'I can't learn. I'm classified such-and-such.'

"We tend to lock children into these learning tracks and there they stay, unless they are lucky enough to get a team who will evaluate them properly and know what they are capable of doing.

"I think your children, Mrs. Sheptock, have helped us to do that—really evaluate and understand other children in the right way.

"Some of the faculty don't understand your faith though. They think you have mystical powers."

I laughed. "Mystical powers? I just rely on God!"

There's no doubt in my mind that part of relying on God is trusting capable and dedicated teachers who want only what's best for the children.

"Mrs. Sheptock, young Mary is making giant strides in seventh grade. She's still immature but is catching up. She takes notes in vocabulary and is always reading. She's not the same hyperactive young woman she was a short time ago.

"Oh, we still see an occasional flare of temper or find her fabricating a story but nothing like it once was."

It thrills my heart to hear reports like that.

We've had young Eric for four years now and his adoption papers are final. When he came to us he had undergone two cranial operations; he was neurologically impaired. His EEG was grossly abnormal and he was very slow in responding to questions, making his speech seem slurred at times. He was also on medication to control his epilepsy.

He loves to sing. And he loves to show off his glasses, especially when he's just gotten new ones.

The children treat it as a special occasion when one of their number is adopted, and it is a special time indeed. When Mary Margaret was adopted we took all the children with us and they lined up, sitting on the front bench of the courtroom, like a row of stairsteps.

"How do you expect to take care of one more child, Mr. Sheptock?" the judge asked.

"These are God's children, your honor. He tells us to take them and He provides what we need."

Some people find this hard to believe. "There's got to be an angle," a real estate man said when he came through the house one day and saw Rudy in baseball cap, football jersey and shorts.

"What's the angle? Nobody could do this out of the goodness of his heart."

"No angle," Rudy told him. "We take the kids that come and God provides."

I guess that man finally believed, for he came back again and brought his wife and even told a friend about us. Not long after that he sent us a large check and so did his friend. We accepted it with thanks, just as we do everything and everybody God sends.

Sometimes He sends more than people. Little Matthew had been asking his father for a pony.

"A pony? We can't afford a pony, Matthew."

It must have been meant for our little boy to have a pony, for one day a friend of Rudy's said he knew where Rudy could buy one at a reasonable price.

"No, Bill, I can't buy a pony. If God wants the kids to have a pony, He'll have to send one."

Two Sundays later Rudy was washing his hands in the men's washroom at church. A fellow turned to him and said, "Do you know anybody who'd take a couple of ponies off my hands?"

OUR GROWING FAMILY

Rudy dried his hands and said casually that he believed he could use them. Other animals have come in by twos, just like they did with Noah's ark. Someone gave us two sheep, two goats and rabbits.

I tried to remember to be thankful when one day the goats kept jumping over the fence. After the third time I told myself, "God sent these goats to us. I have to accept them!" It was then that they stopped jumping out.

Somebody made up a poem about the animals; the kids got a big kick out of it. It went like this:

Because he was hungry,
Domino the goat,
Ate a tin can
And it stuck in his throat.

Penny the pony
Called Alice the sheep,
They took the can out,
And rocked him to sleep.

Lassie the collie
Was barking for joy,
And woke up Domino,
Who then ate a toy!

I'm afraid Robert shocked a friend of ours when he called her and said, "Mrs. Pasqualone, we have five new babies!"

He could almost hear her gasp on the other end of the line.

Baker's Dozen

"Five did you say? Five?"

"Yes, five. Lassie just had puppies!"

She probably wouldn't have been too surprised if we'd just taken in five more children though. She knows us pretty well.

People are always asking how we keep track of so many children. Even Merlyn asked me that when she came over one day.

"When I first knew you I wondered how in the world you kept track of all the children. Remember I asked if you ever misplaced any of them?"

"Sure, I remember how I bragged to you that I never lost track of one for a single minute, remember that? Sure enough the very next week while we were still in Chester we couldn't find Matthew and Mary Claire one day. Rudy and I looked everywhere. It was getting late and we were really worried. Then just by chance he looked in the big doghouse we had and there they both were, fast asleep! Luckily, the dog never used it.

"I was shopping at the grocery store another day and thought I had the children in the car, sitting among the sacks of groceries. I'd already started the car when the check-out lady came running out after me and said, 'Lady, isn't this your child?'

"Mary Margaret had been wandering around the store and I hadn't missed her. Now we double-check every time!"

For some reason Merlyn seemed eager to reminisce that day and we had a good laugh over some of the things that had happened while we were neighbors in Chester.

"Merlyn, do you remember the Jehovah's Witness

fellow who came to my door and I'd just had my new encounter with Christ and couldn't stop talking about it?"

"I remember."

"I must have bowled him over with my testimony and telling him about God's plan for his life. And remember how he ran out of the house and met his friend coming out of your house as upset as he was because you'd been talking the same way?"

Merlyn laughed. "And the one who left my house ran outside and told the fellow coming out of your house, 'Don't go in there. She's a Jesus freak!' Then the other one answered, 'So is this one!'"

Before she left we had made plans to go together to my sister Jeanette's the next day for a Bible study and prayer meeting.

Looking at all the laundry I was folding, Merlyn said she was going to start praying that I would get some help. I assured her I was doing fine and wasn't in the least bit tired but she didn't seem convinced.

Sure enough, when it came time to pray the next day, that's just what she prayed about—that I would get some help with the children.

It was a Thursday morning that will always stand out in my mind, for while we were praying for Merlyn's husband, Rollie, he called to tell her they were being transferred back to Georgia.

The floor could have opened up and swallowed her and I wouldn't have been more surprised or hurt. I couldn't believe it.

"Georgia! Merlyn, tell me it's not true."

"It's true all right. We'll be leaving in a couple of

months."

I cried when I told Rudy about their leaving. He felt badly about it too and put his arm around me, trying to comfort me.

"God will send you another friend, Joanne."

I knew God could do anything, but it still hurts when your best friend is leaving you.

That night before I went to bed I did a thing I haven't done in years, since my convent days, I suppose. I wrote a prayer to God.

"Thank you, Lord, for my friend Merlyn. She was always ready to listen to me talk about you no matter what time of day or night. So many revelations about Jesus that she already knew and yet because of your love and grace, with such a sweet spirit, she listened as if she were hearing them for the first time.

"I know, Lord, that you sent her into my life so that I would see Jesus and come to know and love Him as my personal Savior, as my Lord and Master. I praise you and thank you, Lord.

"O Lord, you know how much I love her and will surely miss her but I know that all things work together for good for those who love the Lord.

"Thank you for your Word. Without it I would have no life. Jesus said, 'I came not only that you might have life but that you might have it abundantly.'

"Praise God!"

11

God's Provisions

When Joanne told me Merlyn was moving away I knew what a gap it would leave in her life. I wondered how in the world the Lord would fill that gap. The two of them had been together so much that they were more like sisters than friends. I'd seen how much Joanne had grown spiritually in the past two years. I saw a difference in both of them actually. Joanne had become more reserved, Merlyn more outgoing, less shy. God had certainly set a good thing going when he sent Merlyn's family to New Jersey. We were fond of them all—Merlyn, her husband, the children. No doubt God had another job for them to do in Georgia but I privately wondered who would be Joanne's helper and confidante now. Physically, I thought she was looking very tired.

I didn't have as much time to help out as I did before I took the new job with Mountain Lakes School System. After eighteen years in my old job I thought it would be hard to adjust to a new situation.

It wasn't. I was just busier, that's all. Lots of work needed to be done in the maintenance line in the new schools.

I met with the school administrators one afternoon and heard them complaining that they had no one to coach the girls' softball team and the girls were insisting on having one.

I sat there listening to all the reasons why they couldn't hire a coach, mainly because it wasn't in the budget. Before I knew it I held up my hand and told the principal that I'd be glad to coach the team. I'd had plenty of experience in sports and I loved it.

"Would you do that, Rudy?" the athletic director asked.

"Sure, if you want me to."

I told him some of the things I'd done: basketball and soccer in high school, basketball in the navy, track and so on.

"Hey, that's great. I'll get back to you on it right away."

He called me a few days later to say, "Rudy, if you still want to coach the softball team, it's a deal."

I had always wanted to be a coach and now I had my chance. There were sixty girls on the high school varsity team. One of the girls sent me a letter when school was out in June of 1976, and it probably tells better than I can what kind of relationship we had.

Dear Mr. Sheptock:
Thank you so much for coaching our softball team. We really appreciate all the time and patience you gave us. Thank you also for creating those trophies. They just show other people what a thoughtful guy you are. Any other coach would have mentioned that he wished there was a trophy for such and such

because she deserves it or something like that. I really appreciate it.

I really think that this season is one I will never forget and with some luck, I hope I'll participate in a few more seasons. We got shellacked in more than one game and yet the team held together. We even got closer as the season progressed. I am sure the primary factor for keeping things going was you. You never raised your voice, not once! (And I even yelled at Jenny a few times.)

My mom kept saying she thought you must be a saint, and that if your car were in anyone else's hands it wouldn't even roll downhill. I think she's right (she always is, anyway).

You left an imprint on my life that I am not likely to forget. Your patience and dedication inspire me. I feel that I'm speaking for the rest of the team as well. No one outside the team knows how much you taught us, but we do.

God bless you and your family,
Betsey M.
P.S. I hope that all of you have a great summer.

Betsey's mother was probably right about my old car. It would hardly roll downhill even for me. It's seen us through many a mile in safety. I can recall several times when if it had not been for God's angels watching out for us, we'd have all ended up in a heap.

The first time was when Joanne was taking some of the children to Kessler Institute in East Orange, New Jersey. All of a sudden the car's engine began smoking and Joanne pulled over immediately. A man in a truck yelled, "Get out of the car, lady. You're on fire!"

Joanne stayed in the car because the Lord told her not to worry. She prayed and the smoke seemed to diminish. A Mercedes pulled up in front of her, a man got out, walked across the street to a gas station. He spoke with the attendant and they both walked back and pushed them into the gas station. She didn't have time to thank the man in the Mercedes before he was gone.

He had been sent by God. Joanne felt he was an angel so she thanked God and asked Him to thank the man for her.

The battery cable had caught fire and the mechanic said it would take a couple of days to repair it as some parts were badly damaged.

Joanne got a ride home and called to tell me. After work that day I took my Uncle Vincent, an auto mechanic, over to the station to look it over. He couldn't find much wrong with it and got it operating in a short time. Then we drove it home.

The second time our car received a "healing" was on a Sunday afternoon when we took all the children—we had about twenty then—in two cars and drove to a seventy-two-acre farm in Pennsylvania. The farm was run by a man and his wife who operate a child care center. He had invited us down for a visit and to talk about how we managed with our young folks.

"Rough Edge Farm" was a beautiful place. Lots of big shady trees, grassy lawns and gardens and so much space for children to play. We met a lot of the kids, and I took some of them out under one of the big, old oak trees and had a talk with them. We had a great time that day. It's

God's Provisions

not often that we get invited out "all together."

It was on our trip back home that we had car problems. The car I was driving began to pull in one direction and I couldn't right it no matter how hard I steered. I signaled to Rudy, Jr. who was driving the rear car and we pulled into the next gas station to ask a mechanic to look it over.

After a short wait he told us, "It may be your universal joint, mister. Looks like it. But you can probably make it home if you're careful."

We started off again. We hadn't gone far until I heard a hissing noise and felt one of the tires go flat. I pulled over to the side of the road and Rudy pulled up in back of me.

He jumped out of the car. "What's wrong now, dad?"

"I think I've got a flat tire. Sounded like it. Felt like it."

We looked all around and none of the tires were flat.

"I really thought we had a flat, son," I told him as we all piled back into the cars.

Back home I had my uncle examine it and he said, "It's not your universal joint, Rudy. What you've got is a broken axle! I don't know how in the world you made it home. It could have collapsed at any time."

Could have—but didn't. Angels were at work, remember?

There was an earlier accident, not in that car, but one involving Joanne and five of the children when they were quite a bit smaller. That was maybe seven years ago when she was taking them to Grandpop Tedesco's for a birthday party. Coming home, rounding a slight curve, she met another car coming from the opposite direction on her side of the road. Swerving to avoid hitting the car, she ran into a tree and then a utility pole, completely totaling the car and smashing the front end. No one was hurt, not even the smallest child.

That was seven years ago. God's provisions are still going strong. Did you know He cares about the smallest detail of our lives? He does.

We had just passed through a very hard winter. It was extremely cold and our house needed insulation as well as other repairs but money was in short supply very often as more children arrived.

One Sunday we woke to find the pipes had frozen in two of the six bathrooms. I knew I couldn't get a plumber on Sunday, and couldn't afford one anyway. I went upstairs and sat on the floor and laid my hands on the frozen pipes. I started to pray. I must have prayed for an hour at least.

"God, we need help today. These pipes are frozen and I can't afford to call a plumber. I know you care about every detail in our lives. I know you can melt this ice. I ask you to do that in the name of Jesus."

I finished praying and got up. Then I heard a faint trickle of water. Drip—drip—drip. It got steadier so I knew the pipe was free. I went downstairs and laid my hands on the pipes in that bathroom, praying for another hour. I smiled as I heard the first slow trickle of water. God had done it again. I thanked Him with tears in my eyes.

When school vacation rolled around that summer I knew I'd have to do something about painting the house. It needed several repairs but I just didn't have the money. I had learned to make do and use ingenuity and common

God's Provisions

sense (in lieu of adequate supplies) during the many years I'd been maintenance supervisor for the schools. In other words, I had learned to do a lot with a little. I'm forever grateful to the two jobs that helped me learn this, and I'm thankful to God for enabling me to fix almost anything from boilers to barber shears.

When your house needs painting, however, there's not too much you can substitute for paint. Instead of painting my own house because I lacked the money, I painted somebody else's house who called up and offered me a job.

I said okay. Then I wondered what price I should ask because the man had wanted to know. I had no idea of what to say. I felt impressed to say, "Whatever God lays on your heart to pay."

God was teaching me to trust Him for all our needs; therefore, whatever he said would be sufficient.

He paid me a nice sum. I was just about ready to buy the paint for our house when a good friend, Ray Tamburello, drove up and said, "Rudy, the Lord has told me to spray paint your house."

He and some people from the Bible study group painted the whole thing and all I had to do was paint the trim. God had provided again.

Earlier we were greatly surprised when a man drove up in a truck and unloaded several bundles of shingles. Somebody had arranged to put a new roof on the house. That's really providing!

Daily, God was showing us that the more we trusted Him the more He would provide. Our Friday night Bible studies began to be proof of that.

When I heard some of the deep discussions that went on

during those times, I realized there was so much I didn't know about the Bible and maybe other subjects as well. I'd never before felt a lack in my life because I didn't go on to college when I had the chance. I had expected to enroll in Oklahoma A. and M. back in 1954, having received a scholarship, but my plans changed.

After I was mustered out of the navy I had several months to wait. My brother was afraid I'd get bored or lazy lying around the house so he sent me out to the Ford plant in Mahwah, New Jersey, to look for a job.

"Rudy, it's no good your hanging around the house until September. They're hiring people in Mahwah. Why don't you apply?"

"I don't know anything about putting cars together, Johnny. What could I do?"

"Don't know, but for two dollars and twenty-seven cents an hour you can sure learn!"

I applied at the Ford plant. They wanted to know what department I wanted to work in. Since I didn't know anything about any department I decided to say "metal finishing." They told me to stand in line with the other applicants as they were being tested to see how much they knew. I stood in line, watching carefully as each man ahead of me ran his hands over the metal surface, feeling for bumps in the paint. I guess it looked like I knew what I was doing, for I followed suit and got the job.

I was making good money for 1954, enough that I soon got myself a new car. I never made it to college because it was hard to give up a steady paycheck and independence.

Leaving there a couple of years later I went back into baking, working at a wholesale pastry shop until I went to

God's Provisions

work at St. Mary's Hospital in Passaic where I met Joanne. I was head man of the coffee shop. I always got nervous when this pretty, dimpled, brunette nurse walked in and I burned many a chop or steak for that reason. It wasn't necessary to have a college degree to do that!

Joanne studied at Seton Hall University in East Orange after we got married in 1959. She came home one evening from working at All Souls Hospital in Morristown and said that this beautiful, little lady, Mary Bobeck, wanted her to teach nursing arts. She said Joanne could get her teaching degree by attending Seton Hall two evenings a week. She already had several college credits from her studies in the convent, so she agreed to do it.

First, Joanne had been a staff nurse, then a head nurse. She always went right to the top because she was a hard worker. I took her to Seton Hall the Saturday she was to take the entrance test. While I waited for her in the lobby I looked at a magazine. It seemed to me I'd no sooner glanced through it than she was back down again. I jumped up.

"What's the matter, Joanne? Didn't you take the test?"

"Oh, sure. I'm finished already."

She was always that way—smart, quick, ready to learn. She took a cardiac course and made the second highest grade in the class. Joanne's a very brilliant girl. I know she viewed her leaving the convent as a failure but she's succeeded in doing a beautiful job as a wife and mother. She's a very special person.

Anyway, I never expected to have the time or money to go to college after losing my chance. I just prayed, "Lord, teach me more."

I was in for a big surprise. A Presbyterian pastor I had met, named Bill Iverson, asked me one day if I'd like to go to New York Theological Seminary and take some courses.

"It's all paid for, Rudy. How about it?"

He had made an offer I couldn't refuse so I went on Saturdays. I was in a class with all pastors. We had to read chapters in systematic theology and in shepherding, and had to write papers on the Bible and answer questions. While I studied at home I usually played Christian records and everything seemed to become so clear as I wrote.

When I handed in my papers, the professor wouldn't believe they were written by a layman. Every week the Lord did it, helping me with my assignments, teaching me more. Some of the weekends we spent in Newark witnessing on the streets. I had earned six credits which would have helped me get into King's College or Northeastern Bible College but I felt the Lord telling me He needed me more on the job at home. I was in danger of becoming a little prideful and He knew it.

I believed He had put me in charge of twenty children and they needed the old man at home. I confined my study to going to church on Sunday, reading the Bible and other books, and going to prayer meetings during the week. The Holy Spirit continued to be the best teacher of all.

People of all ages and all denominations continued to gather on Friday evenings at our house for Bible study and sharing time. They came from all over, twenty-five or thirty each week. One night there were two families here

God's Provisions

from Michigan who knew each other but neither of them knew the other was coming to New Jersey, much less to the Sheptock home. Because of the way God was working in our hearts and home at this time, many people were hearing about our family. We were able to open the door to anyone He would send, whether it be to join our family permanently or just to stay for a short time.

It wasn't only youngsters who came to us for help. Sometimes even adults stayed with us if they were in need. A woman who was having trouble with alcohol, smoking, a bad temper and gossip had been recommended to a Christian organization in south Jersey but she said she'd prefer to come to us. Joanne and I, and other friends as well, worked with her and prayed with her. When she left she was like a different person. She had turned her problems over to God and He had taken care of them. I don't recall Him ever restricting His love and mercy to children only.

A young woman, about twenty-six years old, had come to visit us a couple of times, once with two other girls we knew and once by herself. She never had much to say. We knew from her friends that she wanted to work with children. She seemed to be very lonely and searching for something.

On her second visit, she mentioned she wanted to move into an apartment of her own and take in foster children. Joanne suggested, "Why don't you move in with us?"

"No, I need to live alone!" she replied.

During the course of our conversation, without knowing why, Joanne asked her to move in with us two more times. Both times, she said no and Joanne told her to go home and pray about it.

On the way to her friend's house that afternoon, she realized she would be moving in with us. A week later she called to ask if we really meant what we said about moving in.

Joanne turned to me and asked, "Is it okay?"

I said, "God's kids come in all ages. Let her come."

Joanne reached over and gave me a kiss. "Congratulations! You're about to be a father again!"

When Joanne had assured the young girl that we did want her to come, she laughed and said she'd be there the following Sunday. We had wanted to paint the room first and move the furniture, but she said she would do that herself. Only God and His grace could give this girl the desire to do this.

It was time for me to be a father once again, here at the end of summer. Maybe because I was getting older I began to think about time and seasons. I feel that everything has its season. It's the same with giving and caring. There has to be a time of rest and refilling or a person goes stale. For that reason I was glad to see Joanne invited to a weekend retreat at a Christian center in the mountains of Pennsylvania.

It was a strange Sunday afternoon. Rudy, Jr. and I were sitting in the library watching television. Mary Claire and Mary Christine ran in and out, playing a game of some kind. Eric was doing his homework in the living room with Mary Elizabeth helping him. Young Mary was upstairs playing records and Mary Frances was studying out on the side porch. Mary Ann was on the telephone. Big kids, little kids came in, went out, came in

God's Provisions

again, but we were used to a lot of traffic and it didn't bother us.

Joanne and Merlyn had returned from the retreat late the night before and now Joanne was fixing a farewell dinner for Merlyn and Rollie. Some other friends had come to say good-by to them. They started to come in, then some other people entered and we began to lose track of who was who.

We heard a noise in the front hall and four people came in with bags and boxes, suitcases, tennis rackets and a ladder. They went upstairs.

"Who's that, dad?" young Rudy wanted to know.

"I don't know, son."

Jenny, a young woman who had been staying with us, came downstairs with her belongings, ending her visit. Just then another stranger went up with more boxes and some books. We heard hammering upstairs. A young girl came through carrying a bunch of coat hangers.

"Who's that, Rudy?"

"I don't know, dad."

We had seen the young girl who was planning to move in with us going up and down the stairs with some friends. For a while though it had looked like a Mack Sennett comedy—people going up with ladders, coming down with boxes, borrowing a screwdriver, trying not to step on Frankie and Matthew. One man's family, getting bigger by the minute.

Merlyn, who was going back to Georgia that very day, said a prayer of thanksgiving at dinner.

She said to Joanne, "This girl is the answer to my prayer. God has sent you someone to help you, someone who really loves the children."

Yes, it had been a strange Sunday afternoon. Yesterday our oldest child had been Michael, seventeen and in school in North Dakota. Today our oldest child was a slim slip of a girl, aged twenty-six.

This young girl, who changed her name to Mary Grace, became our next adopted child. It looked for a while as if the state laws wouldn't permit us to adopt her. Unless there was a fifteen-year difference between the ages of the adoptive parents and the child, it wasn't allowed. I fit into the proper age difference okay but Joanne didn't.

Just to show you that with God nothing is impossible, the state laws changed and Mary Grace became the first person to be adopted under the new ten-year law in New Jersey.

She has an interesting story to tell, this older daughter of ours. I think she should tell it herself.

12

Mary Grace

It's a miracle that I ever found my way to Peapack, New Jersey, since I've lived most of my life in Michigan and upstate New York. It seems like such a long journey now that I think of it and it happened in such a roundabout way, but I was looking for a family and sometimes we have to take the long way home.

From the time I was thirteen I was always looking for a mother. I was hungry for family ties and security. My parents were divorced when I was quite young. I don't remember meeting my father until I was sixteen. My mother married four times and I have three sisters from the different marriages. Each time something happened to her marriages I became more insecure. I never really knew what a family was.

When I was sixteen I had gotten very angry at my mother and decided I wanted to go to California and visit my real father. I wrote to him and he sent me a ticket to come out. I only got a one-way ticket because I thought I might decide to stay there.

My father had married again and had several children

by his second wife. I got along all right with the family and stayed for several months although I really had no feeling about wanting to stay indefinitely with my father. My mother wrote that she needed me because my stepfather had died, so I went home again.

The next time I saw him was ten years later when my biological sister asked me to be present when she met our father for the first time. I was surprised at her reaction when she met him. She cried and ran to meet him, giving him a hug. She had always appeared to me to be so strong and independent that I was surprised she would express her true feelings. Although she had been married and divorced and was the mother of two little children, she was as insecure as I was and he represented to her all the security she lacked. I knew his wasn't the love I was seeking.

When I was nineteen sadness and depression were so ingrained in me that I thought there was no way out. Life looked hopeless and I decided to commit suicide. It's a strange feeling, planning to take your own life. I believed that there was a heaven and a hell and I knew that if I committed suicide I would end up in hell but I was determined to do it anyway. I deliberately put thoughts of what might happen afterward out of my mind.

I failed even at suicide. The doctors said they didn't know why I was alive. I should have been dead but I wasn't. I knew God had kept me alive and I was really angry with God that He wouldn't allow me to die.

I was just out of high school after having had a very hard time in school. I got into a lot of trouble, wouldn't study, wouldn't attend classes regularly. I had met a fine

Mary Grace

teacher in high school who was a Christian. I loved to be with her. She tried to tell me about Jesus and I'd listen but I didn't actually want to hear about Jesus, I just wanted to be with this wonderful woman. You see, I was looking everywhere for a mother—everywhere—but she couldn't give me all the time I wanted. I needed a full-time mother.

I started college in Vermont and this teacher called me while I was there, asking me if I wanted to go to a Christian conference in New York City. I didn't especially want to go but I wanted to be with her so I said, "Yes, I'd really like to go."

After I had attempted suicide she had told me she wasn't going to see me or talk to me any more because it was upsetting her family. Besides, it didn't seem to help me anyway. So I was surprised to get a phone call from her. I made plans and flew to New York City, meeting my friend at a Faith at Work conference.

That was the weekend I gave my life to Jesus Christ, struggling against it all the while. I saw that God was revealing himself to me through miracles all weekend.

There was a woman present who had been a heroin addict. I heard her testimony and was very much impressed. I asked her if I could talk with her and she said yes, so we met for breakfast the next morning.

I had seen a lot of drinking in my life, also sex and abuse and I had gotten involved with drugs myself. It seemed pretty fantastic that someone like this woman could have her whole life cleaned up and changed by believing in Jesus Christ.

The weekend was coming to a close. At the final gathering there was an invitation to anyone who wanted to give their lives to Jesus. I sat there, shaking inside, knowing I would have to put my hand up, not knowing if I could do it. I couldn't. Because I was so insecure I couldn't raise my hand and go to the front of the room.

The meeting closed and I sat there in that big room which would hold about a thousand people. Everyone had gone but me. I felt as if I had missed my chance. It was that cold, sinking feeling you get as you watch your flight take off without you—that lonely feeling of being left behind.

I wanted to apologize to someone.

I whispered, "Jesus, I really do want you to be my Savior."

I don't know if that's the moment when He came into my life but I think it was. I knew at that point that Jesus was real. God allowed me to see that.

There were still a lot of things in my life He had to change after that. I was drinking and doing drugs at the same time I was earnestly seeking Christian fellowship.

I'd gone to a couple of different colleges—Green Mountain College in Vermont and Cortland State College in New York. After graduating from Cortland and getting a degree in sociology, I sent out several applications. I hadn't heard from any of them until a couple of months later when I got a call from a man in New York City who said he knew someone in East Orange, New Jersey, who might be interested in my qualifications. He gave me a couple of addresses where I could write.

About a month later I received a call from the Salvation Army in East Orange asking me to come for an interview. He had three different job openings.

Mary Grace

I called a friend in Staten Island who agreed to go with me. I also called my former teacher and asked her to pray for me about it. I said if they offered me a job I would feel it was God's leading.

My friend from Staten Island and her parents took me to East Orange for the interview. It lasted about two hours. All this time the man still hadn't offered me a job.

Finally I asked, "Are you offering me a job or aren't you?"

He said, "You can have any of these three jobs we've discussed."

I chose the job I thought I could do best and agreed to be back in New Jersey within two weeks.

Although I had accepted the job I still wasn't sure I should go. Here, where I was living, I had some security and a few friends I could trust. I hated to venture out into the unknown by myself. It was a big step and I didn't know if I could make it.

As I walked around the apartment wondering what to do, still in Cortland on the very day I was supposed to be in New Jersey, I experienced the presence of God in a way I have never known. It was a sense of the sternness of God. I could literally feel His presence.

He seemed to be telling me, "If you don't go now, there's nothing more I'll be able to do for you. If you don't go where I have opened a door for you—"

I don't know if I felt I would be cut off forever but I certainly knew that I needed to get going. I threw my things in my car and left.

I'd never been to New Jersey except for the trip I made for the interview. I hardly knew where to begin to look for an apartment so it was a relief to find that I could share an apartment with another girl who also worked for the Salvation Army. My job only lasted six months, then I got laid off.

I then took a job in Newark doing accounts receivable. This, too, only lasted for six months. Soon after, my roommate and I both went to work for a book publishing company in Plainfield, New Jersey. We moved into a two-bedroom apartment with two other girls and began attending a church in Plainfield which we liked right from the start. This was 1973.

On the surface it looked as though I was quite well-adjusted but I wasn't. I was still terrified of close relationships, at the same time I was desperately searching for just that. Inside I had the same old insecure feelings.

This became evident when my friend from East Orange decided to move out of the apartment and get a place in another town with another friend of ours. I felt deserted all over again. My two best friends were moving together without me. The two of them had found a house they liked and moved to Peapack, New Jersey. I had never heard of Peapack before. In all of this, I believe God was teaching me to depend on Him. Although my two closest friends had gone, He would remain with me.

I stayed on in the apartment for another year, sharing it with two other roommates. They never seemed to get along well, and one or the other of them was always thinking of moving. First one would mention looking for another place, then the other, so that I was constantly frightened that I would be left alone. I knew I hadn't enough money to keep the apartment by myself and I dreaded the thought of trying to make new friends, of living with new people.

Hoping to escape further conflict, I changed jobs in the company, taking one that allowed me to work nights. This I liked, working in the computer room, with only one other person on duty. Then in the daytime I had the apartment to myself. I needed this time alone because God was doing some deep inner healing in my life and I couldn't have faced a lot of people.

On a visit to my friends' home in Peapack, they told me about a family they had met which they thought I would like to know. This family had a lot of adopted children, many of them handicapped. I had often expressed a desire to work with such children, for I just seemed to have an in-built empathy for children with problems. I thought I might like to visit the family.

On the day I planned to go, no one was available to go with me. Since I hated going anywhere by myself, especially where I was to meet new people, it was really surprising that I went at all. But I did, and I guess I must have acted strangely.

I didn't say much, just went through the house, with one of the children showing me around. I saw the mother giving the father a haircut and I thought, "How weird."

They told me later I looked pretty weird myself. I had on old dungarees and a plaid shirt, with a very short haircut. I don't even remember how I looked and I probably didn't much care. I do remember we sat in the library and Mrs. Sheptock did most of the talking. Her friend, Merlyn, sat on the couch and didn't say very much. I stayed for about an hour and left. I visited once more after that when Mrs. Sheptock asked me to come live with them.

I was amazed at the peace God had given me and I knew that afternoon that I would move in, but I didn't call again for at least a week.

There was still much insecurity in my life. I had made a decision but I was never really sure I had made the right choice. God was so good; He opened all the doors, worked out the insecurities, the hurts, and the fears in His timing. I knew I wanted to have a mother and father and lots of brothers and sisters whom I could love and from whom I could receive love. That was the way they wanted it too.

That's my mom and dad, opening their arms and hearts to their seventeenth child—me. I was home at last, praise God! Soon to be joined by more brothers and sisters.

13

Be Patient With Me, Mommy

For six months after Mary Grace came to live with us we had no little babies in the house so I had lots of time to get acquainted with my new daughter. This was good because she needed lots of understanding and acceptance in addition to motherly love. With the two of us shopping for groceries, doing laundry and getting the children off to school, I had more time to relax than I'd had in a long while.

I remember saying to Merlyn when she left, "What am I going to do with all this love?"

I should have known it wouldn't be long before more little ones would come to claim it. Our youngest ones at that time were a trio of four-year-olds, Matthew, Frankie and Mary Christine and a duet of three-year-olds, Mary Claire and Marty. Marty was three when he came to us, a very lovable little fellow. He became legally ours within a few months after Mary Grace arrived.

Hazel-eyed Marty needs lots of help, though there are many things he can do for himself. Marty is a Down's syndrome child.

OUR GROWING FAMILY

I had often wondered what I would do if I ever had a Mongoloid child. I can remember thinking about that a long time ago. Then, when we were called to take Marty, we didn't even see him in advance.

We were supposed to meet him in another town because the family who had him could no longer keep him and the agency had arranged for us to meet so that we could see him first. There was some sort of mix-up in transportation and he never arrived.

We told the agency, "That's okay. We'll take him anyway." So we did.

Between December of 1976 and March of 1977 the Sheptock family increased by two new babies—Jon, six months old and Timmy, three months old.

Jon is a beautiful, red-haired charmer. With deep blue eyes and a sweet smile, young Jon was born without arms. We all fell in love with him immediately.

He cried much at night in the first weeks he was with us. Mary Grace and I took turns rocking him and comforting him. The kids fuss over who is going to feed him. He's a lover in many ways, being especially fond of small children and dogs. He stands on my lap and dances to music on television. He likes to watch the cartoons with the smaller children.

One of the social workers had written us about him.

"It will take a lot of love, care and patience to raise this little boy, but I'm sure he is worth any sacrifice."

She was right. We've accepted Jon as he is. He'll grow up feeling normal one day.

A friend asked me once, "How did you feel the first time you gave him a bath?"

Be Patient With Me, Mommy

The first time I gave him a bath he squealed and laughed when I washed his ears. How did I feel? I just wanted to love him. I knew I'd have to hug him a lot because he couldn't hug back. His mommy would have to hug for two.

I was so excited when I realized Jon would be coming to live with us. There were two other families who had wanted him, so we prayed, "Lord Jesus, if it be your will please give Jon to us." I had prayed for a new baby and Jon was my answer to prayer. When I told people God had answered my prayers and given me a baby, some said, "It's no problem to get children with handicaps. There are lots of those waiting, but to get a perfect one, that's a different story." But I knew different. Jon was my perfect baby. God's purposes would be worked out in his life.

Because of people and their standards I prayed one night for a "whole baby," perfect in people's eyes so they may know that nothing is impossible with God.

It was only two days later when I received a call from Catholic Welfare in Trenton, asking us if we wanted a perfectly healthy, little interracial boy, three months old. I was so excited I could hardly hold on to the phone. How great is our God!

I knew Timmy was an answer to prayer but someone still asked me if I didn't consider a multiracial background a handicap. I replied that I didn't. I believe the only real handicap one has is not to know Jesus and His love for us.

After Timmy arrived we realized God had a two-fold purpose for sending him. One, to show people nothing is impossible with God and God answers prayers. The second purpose was that Timmy and Jon, so close in age, would grow together, attend school together and help one another in whatever ways God would have for them. It just seemed that Timmy was sent to be Jon's arms when he needs them. There they were, almost the same age, and they would undoubtedly be in the same grades in school. Timmy, being a boy, would be able to help Jon with buttons and zippers and things he couldn't manage.

I was delighted to read that attention is being paid to the designing of clothes for handicapped children, eliminating hard-to-open-and-close zippers and buttons, streamlining clothes to suit their particular needs. That's real progress in teaching young children to be independent and self-sufficient within their limitations, and I'm all for that. These special little ones need to be cared for tenderly and taught so much.

When we went to get our little boy, Timmy, one of the papers they gave us had the following paragraph that I thought I would like to share with all parents:

> In the sight of God, your work is that wondrous task of being a real father and mother. It is an important task. It comes before your health and your wealth. It comes before your success and your ease. It comes before your personal desires and your talents. It is a tremendous task, but God give you His grace and the power to love, and with these you will be able to fulfill your responsibilities. . . .

It's an awesome thing to be a parent. But to try to raise children without the knowledge and love of God should be a terrifying thought to us. It should make us love our

Be Patient With Me, Mommy

children more and teach them who their heavenly Father is. Every day I am grateful that our older children know what their spiritual inheritance is.

Mary Ann and Mary Frances, sixteen and fifteen, are so good to help with the new ones. They will make good mothers themselves someday. There was a time when Mary Ann had some difficulties sharing her mother with all of the new children, especially those who required so much care and attention. My heart would almost break each time she got upset but I knew I could trust Jesus and I would pray for her over and over, believing that God would help her, the other children and me and make us more like Jesus, learning to give and give and give. A healing has taken place in her attitude and she is more loving and kind than ever before. In fact, one day I heard her telling one of the little children to have more respect for her father and me. Whoever it was wanted to know what "respect" meant.

"Respect means to be quiet," said Mary Ann, "even when you think you're right." Mary Ann will be attending Nyack Missionary College when she graduates from high school. I'm really happy about her plans to be a missionary, sharing the good news with others.

She's a great athlete, plays basketball and once went on a five-hundred-mile bike trip. She likes to draw and does it very well.

Mary Frances was so eager to help with the children that I found myself keeping her out of school too often. She wanted to help, so I let her. She's a real homebody and is very good with the children. One of the teachers pointed out to me that it was really fine for her to have all those traits but Mary Frances needed her formal education too. I see that now. She'll probably go on to college. Her godmother, Vera, has plans to send her there.

This pretty child, who doesn't always realize she's pretty, has been a strong right arm for her mother but I don't keep her out of school any more. It turned out God had another idea when He sent Mary Grace to us.

After Jon and Timmy came, two more little ones arrived and we woke up one day to realize that our growing family had suddenly become two parents and twenty-one children: Mary Grace, Michael and Rudy; Mary Ann, Mary Frances and Mary; Robert, Mary Elizabeth and Michael Joseph; David, Eric and Mary Margaret; Matthew, Frankie and Mary Christine; Mary Claire, Martin and Jon; Timmy, Ali and Veronica.

How could we have said no to four-year-old Ali, partially blind and partially deaf, who sits in the big, sprawling playpen and rocks back and forth, making soft moaning noises? He's a beautiful child and so is his wee sister, Veronica, nine months old. We took them so their mother could receive rehabilitation from drugs in a program called "New Life for Girls." This is a Christian organization with centers in the United States and abroad. From time to time we get children on a temporary basis through this fine group.

People have wondered if our problems increase as our family gets larger and I guess that's right, but I know our blessings increase in an even greater measure. My

Be Patient With Me, Mommy

biggest problem has always been myself, my needing more patience, needing to understand that children sometimes respond slowly to warmth and affection. When you love, love, love and give, give, give and a child remains passive and unresponsive, it begins to be frustrating.

Eric and I had this problem. Eric, who is now nine, was at first slow to accept his sonship and our love.

People tend to think our life seems unrealistic, full of happy endings. They don't understand that real, actual, day-by-day living goes on in this household just as it does in anyone else's home. Real things happen and I react like any other mother.

Eric and I were upstairs one afternoon and I had corrected him about something. His response had been cold and negative.

"Why, Eric? Don't you feel you're one of the family? Don't you know how much daddy and I love you? Must you always pull away and hold us at a distance?"

His answer was the same old frustrating whine. He was totally unreachable. I lost my patience with him and pushed him. It caught him off balance and he fell forward, knocking out a front permanent tooth. Blood was coming from his mouth and he was crying. I was scared and crying too, trying to pray, with tears streaming down my face.

I picked up Eric and scooped up the tooth from the floor as I ran downstairs. Rudy, Jr. was just coming through the front door.

"What happened, mom?"

I explained quickly, then added, "I can't get him to the dentist until later because I have to go to school and help with the children's physical exams. I had promised. What am I going to do, Rudy?"

He took one look at the bloody tooth, the crying child and the nervous mother. He said, "Let's pray about it, mom."

Feeling weak anyway I sat down on the bottom stair step with Eric in my lap, took the tooth in my right hand and gently but firmly pressed it back into Eric's gum, holding it there while Rudy and I prayed.

I washed us both off, put him in Rudy's care and hurried off to school. I made a quick call to the dentist and asked if I could bring Eric in when I finished at school. He said sure.

It was four o'clock by the time I got him to the dentist's office. He took an X-ray and didn't even touch the tooth.

"Looks fine to me, Mrs. Sheptock. I don't even need to stabilize. Don't do anything to it. I believe it'll be okay."

It was. It's been fine ever since. The dentist didn't even send us a bill. God works through ordinary people oftentimes, using them as His hands and feet here on earth, using them to help work His miracles. I believe in miracles, for I had witnessed one that very day.

So you see I'm not an unusual mother, just ordinary, expecting God to help me with everything. I depend on Him to keep me going. Sometimes when I am tired or at my wit's end and wonder how I can do one more thing for one more person, I open my Bible and read some of His promises. Then I claim one for myself. That way He upholds me daily.

I'm sure God expects more from all of us than we give Him. I know He expects us to follow His leading and tell of

Be Patient With Me, Mommy

the wonderful things He does in our lives. There may be someone right near to us who needs to hear that God is alive and working even today. People need to know that He loves them.

One day I was shopping in the grocery store. Several of the children were with me. I noticed we always seemed to end up in the aisle with one particular woman who had a little boy who was about four years old with her. He kept picking up things to put in the cart and she kept telling him to put them back.

We separated in the cereal aisle but I began to feel a burden to pay the woman's grocery bill. I wasn't sure why. I went to the check-out counter but didn't see her, checked out and started outside, thinking maybe I was wrong. Then I saw her in the parking lot and I knew I had to do it, no matter what she might think.

I stepped up to her and told her I felt God had impressed upon me that I should pay her grocery bill. I had no idea of how much it was, but I asked her name and began to write out a check for the amount she named—ten dollars and twenty-five cents. She just took it and didn't say a word.

That night about eight o'clock the phone rang and it was the same woman. She told me why she'd allowed me to pay her bill. For years she had been a Christian but just a few days before she had decided to trust God completely and she felt this was His way of showing her she was right.

One other time this same thing happened to me while shopping and that woman told me she'd had a daughter who had been miraculously healed of meningitis. That was a day when I needed to hear that miracles still happen. I need to hear about our great God as often as the next person.

People should know that Rudy and I are ordinary parents. Our children behave just as they do in other families, showing off when there's company, taking advantage when they can, quarreling among themselves, testing us to the limit. Meal times can be pretty hectic especially when there's a guest.

On a particular Saturday morning when we had a guest I walked into the library and saw several little bodies curled up on and around a large bean-bag chair on the floor, engrossed in watching a television program called "Wonderbug," about a car that flies, talks and changes character. It was a nice day and the children should have been outside.

Frankie, David and Joey (a temporary guest) were squishing about on the black bean-bag chair. Eric was on the floor on one side of them, Matthew on the other. Jovan, a little boy who was also with us temporarily, was in the kiddie seat by the couch. Timmy was in the playpen, singing to himself, kicking up his heels and playing with the pictures on his red sneakers. Mary Elizabeth came in and sat on the couch by Jovan. Mary Frances brought young Jon in and put him on the floor. I knew they should be outside but I hadn't the heart to disturb them just yet.

Red-haired Jon, having no arms, scoots around on his bottom and isn't always too careful where he scoots. In kicking out his legs to maneuver himself closer to the television set he managed to kick Frankie and David.

Be Patient With Me, Mommy

They promptly paid him back in kind. A free-for-all had just broken out in the library when their father walked in.

Rudy, in his Saturday outfit of red football jersey with the big thirty-eight on it and his old baseball cap, promptly brought them up short. He grabbed Frankie and David, pulling them to their feet.

"What's the idea of hitting Jon? You've hurt him and he's crying!"

"He kicked us first," said David.

"Yes, he did," Frankie agreed.

"Jon kicks because he's only two years old and he's trying to get around. When that happens, don't hit him back! Come and tell me and I'll take care of him."

Frankie and David got a quick spanking each and father proceeded to break up the television-watching by issuing the weekly chore schedule which he proposed to put into practice immediately.

As I went by the door I heard the work detail assignments being made and heard the kids' reactions.

"Okay, kids, here's the schedule for this week and I want you to start right now.

"Frankie, you will clean out the game closet here in the library, sorting out the games, the puzzles and toys.

"Eric, you'll empty the wastebaskets and take out the garbage.

"Michael will dry the silverware and sweep.

"Matthew will clean the stairs. Also Matthew and Frankie will clean under the beds.

"David will dry the dishes."

Several of the children groaned at their assigned tasks. One or two called, "Yay!" when it appeared their lot was to be an easy one. Matthew and Frankie got up to start their work at once but Rudy called them back.

"Wait until I'm finished. You might miss something you're supposed to do. Mary Elizabeth, you're to clean out two coat closets and look after Martin. Okay?"

She nodded.

"Margy, you'll collect the laundry."

"Yuk!" I heard our seven-year-old say.

"Mary Claire will put toilet paper in each bathroom. Mary Christine will collect all the shoes that get left around in the rooms."

I hurried back into the kitchen to start preparing lunch before my eager husband should think of something he'd like me to do that I wasn't already doing.

It takes awhile to prepare a meal and feed our brood even when it's a lunch of cold cuts, rolls and salad, which it was today. Some of the little ones were still on baby food and had to have their lunch in the highchair or kiddie seat. We had to be careful that Martin didn't get tomatoes as he's allergic to them.

The older ones ate quickly and asked to be excused. Robert hurried out to the kitchen to start making the meatballs for supper. He's beginning to enjoy cooking and is a really big help in the kitchen. I noticed he could keep his eye on us and hear what we said in the dining room. He also doesn't like to miss anything.

Bickering had broken out at one end of the table among the young ones as to who should go with Mary Ann when she left to take our guest home and visit a friend on the way. I knew I'd have to go along since Mary Ann was driving on a learner's permit and needed a licensed driver

Be Patient With Me, Mommy

with her.

"Can I go? Can I go?" yelled Frankie.

Margy began to pout. "I never go!"

"The girls go everywhere," said Matthew solemnly.

"We do not!" maintained Margy. "If I stay here with Mary Frances she won't play with me. Can I call Allison, mom? Nobody else likes me! You won't give me part of that peach you're cutting. Nobody likes me!"

Mary Margaret continued her whining until she got herself a spanking and an answer that she couldn't call Allison.

I could hear Rudy in the living room asking someone, "Why did you hit Timmy on the head?"

One of the little boys answered, "Because he was screaming!"

"Well, he's really screaming now. Don't do that again!"

Mary Claire, missing out on the peaches, demanded a doughnut or a lollipop.

"Mary Claire, tell your brother to give you a doughnut. He's in the kitchen making meatballs." I instructed my small daughter.

"Robert won't give me one. He never will."

"Mom, do these pants look okay?" Rudy, Jr. strolled in to have me check his trousers.

"Mother, we have to hurry if I'm to be in Berkeley Heights by three o'clock," Mary Ann rushed in. "Do we have to take Timmy?"

"Yes, we have to take Timmy."

She went off looking not too happy about the prospect of getting him ready to go.

And so it went, a leisurely luncheon at the Sheptocks'.

Happily, not all meals are so hectic. Sometimes the children behave beautifully, say "please" and "excuse me" especially if there's a birthday party coming up. That's one celebration each person in our family is entitled to—a cake for his or her birthday and as much of a party as we can afford. Occasionally a group of young people will come in with half a dozen cakes and several gallons of ice cream and we all have a merry time.

One such group surprised Mary on her fourteenth birthday, bringing her a butterfly necklace and taking pictures. With so many children, there is a birthday quite often. In February, for example, we have five in one week.

Rudy and I were sitting on the back porch one evening in late summer, 1977, talking about who was going to have the next birthday. He reminded me that there would soon be an anniversary—we would have been living in our house for three years. I began to think of the children who'd come and gone, those who'd stayed and of Merlyn who went to Georgia and was still there.

It was a warm night, quiet except for a few crickets in the bushes nearby. Distant lightning played across the sky over the barn. The smell of rain was in the air. Rudy reached over and took my hand.

"I'm glad Mary Grace is here so we can have a little more time together. I like having a daughter her age, don't you? In fact, I'm beginning to feel that we're Abraham and Sarah. You know, in old age our descendants are multiplying like the sands of the sea." (He was forty-five and I was forty.)

I couldn't resist a laugh.

Be Patient With Me, Mommy

"Rudy, you don't know the half of it. You know how Sarah's womb was opened in her old age? Well, so's mine. I'm pregnant!"

He didn't say anything at first. Just sat there, looking at the lightning and the leaves beginning to stir gently on the trees. I wasn't sure he had heard me.

"Oh, I heard you and I think it's great. I wonder if we'll have a boy or girl. It's been so long since I went through paternity this way that I don't know if I've got the patience to wait nine months!"

Ah, patience. Soon there would be one more little one to say, "Be patient with me, mommy. I'll learn someday what I'm supposed to do. I'll surprise you by giving back all your love, your patience and caring, then you'll know that you were doing the right thing. I'll grow up and you'll be proud of me. I promise you."

This imaginary conversation triggered a remembrance of an incident told me by a friend. Her grandmother used to care for a little orphan boy. She was poor and couldn't afford too many luxuries but she often took the boy to the movies because he enjoyed them so much.

At a Saturday matinee he sat through the film, taking everything in, admiring his current hero, a cowboy. The cowboy got off his horse, turned and waved, it seemed, right in the little boy's direction.

Excitedly, the little fellow turned to the grandmother and whispered. "When I'm grown up I'll be a famous movie star. That'll be me up on the screen. Everybody will see me and think I'm waving to them but I'll be waving to you, nana!"

It was his way of showing her how much he loved her. His way of thanking her for her care and patience.

14

A Christmas Celebration

Christmas, 1977, was a happy and exciting time in the Sheptock household on Peapack Road. Snow was everywhere. Rudy had taken great care to cover all the exposed windows with transparent vinyl to help keep out the winter winds. The smaller boys kept shoveling constantly to keep paths open to the barnyard where the ponies, sheep and goats were. In large bags and cans they carried out scraps for the animals to eat and fed them hay and grain.

I was very large with child, expecting our baby near the end of March. How good it was to have Mary Grace, Mary Ann and Mary Frances helping with the children and the household details while the older children were in school.

My big project for this day was to make a large pot of vegetable soup so I carried all the vegetables into the dining room and sat on the long bench at the table, peeling carrots, potatoes, everything from the refrigerator that was "limp." These would go in the soup pot for supper. On cold nights Rudy liked nothing better than homemade soup. He loved to see the big, white tureen in the middle of the table. The children enjoyed it as well.

Mary Christine backed up to me, wanting help with the buttons on her jumper. She was getting ready to go to afternoon kindergarten.

"Mommy, will you button my top button?"

I said sure, and teasingly jabbed her chin. She and I had had a small crisis a few hours earlier. Mary Christine hadn't obeyed in something I'd asked her to do so she had been punished and was still a little pouty.

"Mary Christine, do you think you'll remember when mommy asks you to do something next time, that I mean to do it *now*?"

She nodded solemnly, with her brown eyes wide and very serious. She didn't say anything but slipped her small arm around my shoulders. I knew we were in communication again.

"Okay, honey, now run and help Mary Grace with Jon's snowsuit and they can drop you off at kindergarten on their way to the store."

I patted her brown head and she scooted off.

Mary Claire was talking to baby Timmy, who was still in the highchair in the kitchen. She was scolding him for throwing his spoon on the floor. I got up to take him out of the chair just as the telephone rang. Mary Grace answered it on her way out the door.

"Mommy, it's long distance. Michael is calling. Can you take it?"

I put Timmy in the playpen and picked up the phone.

"Hello, Michael. I'll bet I know why you're calling."

On the other end of the line I heard eighteen-year-old Michael with his deep voice asking how cold and snowy it

A Christmas Celebration

was here. As I expected, he was calling to tell us when his plane would arrive from out West. He was looking forward to the Christmas vacation at home.

We chatted for a few minutes. I went back to soup-making, thinking of Michael and how we had come to have him for the past two years.

Michael, at eighteen, is trying hard to find his identity. He's black, lives his life in a wheelchair and goes to school out-of-state. His legs are atrophied from cerebral palsy but he has good control otherwise. His education, paid for by the state of New Jersey, will equip him to be independent and self-sufficient in a trade he is learning.

How he came to live with us is a very interesting tale. I had left the younger children with a baby-sitter down the street one afternoon, among them our little Mary Margaret, who has one good arm and a prosthesis for the other. For some unknown reason, the head of the cerebral palsy school, Mattheny School in Peapack, stopped at the baby-sitter's house that day. He saw Margy and asked about her and her family.

The sitter told him we had several handicapped children and the head of the school wondered if she'd ask me to call him. I did and later went to the school to visit when the youngsters put on a Christmas play. That's when I met Michael. They told me he needed a place to stay for holidays and during school vacations because he would be away most of the year at school in another state.

At first, Michael found it hard to adjust to the family. Like many children with handicaps, he tended to become wrapped up in himself and his needs, and expected to be catered to and made exception for because of his problems. For a long time we didn't adopt Michael because he didn't wish to be.

During summer vacation of 1978 Michael seemed to be starting to realize that his family really means something to him and he decided he wanted to be adopted. His whole attitude seemed to change. He was more concerned with his dad and mom and his brothers and sisters than he was with himself. Thanks be to God for this change!

Our other Michael, who is eleven years old with congenital blindness, mild cerebral palsy and a low IQ, came to us in August, 1977. Michael had been in one foster home for seven years of his life and two other adoptive placements before coming to our house. I believe Michael, this particular child of mine, was God's instrument used to teach me what real "agape love" is all about. The past year was not an easy one but I would not have traded it for anything.

Before Michael came to our home much of his time had been spent reading, coloring, watching TV and playing with his fire trucks. The first time I saw him I realized he had much more potential than his behavior indicated. It had been dormant because of the lack of challenge or knowledge of his true ability.

He was out of school for five months because we couldn't find an appropriate school for him—one that would not only meet his physical and emotional needs, but would meet his intellectual needs also.

We prayed much for the right school for him, and after five long months, the Lord answered our prayers with a good school in Bernardsville, New Jersey, which had decided to take him on a three-month-trial basis. I was really happy and I knew in my heart Michael could do it with much unwanted encouragement from us, but we were determined to give it to him.

Michael was placed in the regular fourth grade and went for supplemental help in his weakest subjects.

Michael did what we knew he could do. He was able to keep up and remained in this school.

He has had much difficulty doing as he is told. I prayed one night and asked God for a word for Michael. The word that came to me was "insubordinate." When I looked it up I found it meant "rebellious, disobedient." This is a result of rejection and our Michael had experienced much of this. I was able to understand now, but Jesus taught me that I needed not only to understand but I needed to accept Michael (just as he is) and trust Jesus to change him. I knew I couldn't do this, so I told Jesus He would have to do this through me. And although I have difficulty believing it myself sometimes, I know that these are not just words. We must accept people as they are. I am really learning to live and feel and do that.

One little fellow who doesn't let his handicap keep him from enjoying life is our Jon. As soon as he and Mary Grace come home from shopping and he's out of his blue snowsuit, down on the floor he goes, scooting around on his bottom. He examines cabinets, pulling open drawers with his feet and kicking at a soft, red ball. He doesn't let the fact that he has no arms keep him from having fun.

One of his favorite things is singing. Mary Frances has an album of music from the movie *Grease*, and young Jon

OUR GROWING FAMILY

loves it. The other day I saw him sitting on the coffee table where Mary Elizabeth had put him, singing and wiggling his feet.

"What are you singing, Jon?" Mary Elizabeth asked him.

"Singing *'Gwease'* " was his reply.

Cousin Vera says she'll take him to see the movie when it comes around, even if he's barely two. That may even be his birthday present.

A beautiful color picture of Jon, made by the March of Dimes people, hangs on the cedar shakes in the kitchen now. He will be their Northern New Jersey poster boy for 1978-79.

Mary Grace and I put the little ones down for naps, do several loads of laundry, go over final plans for dinner and answer the telephone many times. I get lots of phone calls, many of them quite unexpected. Not long ago a former classmate from nursing school called because she had seen our name in the telephone book. We hadn't seen each other for several years. She has lived in the Midwest for a long time.

It saddened me to hear that she had an unhappy marriage. I don't think she really understood all the things I told her about the children and our way of life. No matter, we'll have lunch together soon and I can tell her everything.

As I write this, the sky is darker and it's beginning to snow quite heavily. I'm glad the little ones will soon be in from school. A mother hen always feels better when the chicks are tucked safely under her wing. They are all

A Christmas Celebration

getting very excited, knowing that Christmas is coming fast. Little packages and gifts they've made in school come home and are hidden in different parts of the house. Nobody's allowed to look at them before Christmas.

There's no more quiet now as the first graders, Matthew and Frankie, arrive. They specialize in noise. Eric shows me his third-grade spelling paper and tells me one of the kids on the bus wonders how Eric, Matthew and Mary Margaret can all be brothers and sisters when they're different colors.

"I don't know what to tell him, mom."

"What you can tell him, Eric, is this. Everybody is a mixture of colors since everybody has two parents. Matthew is white and white. Margy is white and black and you are black and black. Tell him God's children come in all colors and it suits your parents just fine. Does that sound like a good answer?"

Eric laughed and said, "Yeah, mom."

I remember when one of the children was questioning why Jon had no arms. Mary Grace's answer was, "That's God's plan for Jon's life."

It satisfied me and I guess it satisfied the small fry who are learning unerringly that God does indeed have a plan for each of our lives and we should all cooperate with Him in finding out what it is.

Margy, even with one arm, is learning to play the piano. She reported today that her teacher won't be able to give her any more lessons just now. Margy doesn't look too sad about it but I know she enjoys playing.

Perhaps Rudy, Jr. can help her, although he mostly plays by ear. When he isn't playing baseball he's constantly pounding out tunes on the piano. He's composed many songs, probably thirty or more.

It's still snowing heavily and the boys are anxious to start shoveling. Matthew wants to know if they can begin shoveling a path to the animal shed.

"Matthew, the snow hasn't stopped yet. Don't you want to wait until there's more to work with?"

I couldn't convince him that it looked like it might snow for hours so he and Frankie got into their warm jackets, mittens and boots and went outdoors. They probably needed some loosening up after a long day in school. Mary Christine tried to join them but couldn't find an extra shovel so she came back inside and played with Marty.

Rudy, Mary Ann and Mary Frances have come home from their daily train ride to school. In a way it was quite exciting to catch a train to go to school. So far they have managed to make it on time every day.

Rudy made a beeline for the table in the front hallway where we put the daily mail. He was eager to know if he had received an early acceptance from the college he applied to. I knew there was a letter waiting for him since the mail had come at noon. I heard him yell when he opened it.

"Mom, look, look! I made it. They accepted me!"

He came into the dining room where I was helping Mary and Mary Frances set the table for dinner. He waved the letter in my face.

"See, I'm in! It's all settled."

I read the letter he handed me. Sure enough, the Philadelphia College of Bible had sent him an early acceptance. This is the first step in his preparation for

A Christmas Celebration

Christian ministry.

"You know, mom, I'm really glad I know where I'm going."

He stopped in the kitchen and patted me on the shoulder.

"I'm glad too, Rudy. Your dad will be also." I gave him a quick kiss on the cheek, happy that he wasn't too old or too tall to accept it.

"That's a good Christmas present, son. One we won't have to wrap." Before I finished the sentence he was off to call his friend Joel on the telephone. Good news must be shared!

I hadn't done any Christmas shopping in three years. I had just asked the Lord to provide what we needed. He always has. The first Christmas we were in this house we had no money to buy gifts but many presents came in for the children. The second year it was even bigger and better. I knew God wouldn't fail us this year.

That very evening, after the dinner dishes were washed and we were getting the little ones ready for bed, young people from Long Hill Chapel came with a big, green tree with snowflakes in its branches, which they set up in a corner of the living room. Bedtime was forgotten as the children crowded around to watch them take trimmings out of boxes.

The children were each given something to put on the tree—a shiny ball, a bell, colored rings and strings of lights. It was probably the biggest and best Christmas tree we have ever had.

The people from the chapel have been so good to us on many occasions. It was they who sent us the first

OUR GROWING FAMILY

fifty-dollar gift when we moved here, signifying God's desire to provide and care for us.

Rudy and I sat down by ourselves in the living room to enjoy looking at the tree after the children had gone off to bed. We talked about what we'd cook for Christmas dinner and who we might expect to come. On holidays we usually had a few extra guests, not all of them relatives. One older woman comes who has no family to be with at holidays.

We expected fifteen-year-old Billy to be back with us for Christmas.

The children have two living grandparents—my father and Rudy's mother, living in California. Neither of them will be here for Christmas dinner.

My sister Jeanette will come before Christmas and give all the girls haircuts. Being a hairdresser, she gives us the latest styles and we feel so neat afterwards. Rudy's brothers and sister and their families will come sometime during the holidays but not for Christmas Day. That day they like to spend with their own families.

So the wintry days hurry by as we bundle up and wait for the celebration of the birthday of God's Son, Jesus. Even the youngest of our crew understands to some degree what the celebration is all about. To Ali, who cannot see or hear well, we can only communicate this wonderful event by loving him. We've just heard that Ali and his little sister Veronica will soon leave us for Pennsylvania to be nearer their mother in her rehabilitation program. She loves the children, so we know it will be all right.

Their beds won't stay empty for long. There are always

little birdlings who have no nest. It may be that God will send them here so that we may help them learn to fly.

Good smells come from the kitchen these days as Mary Grace, Mary Ann, Mary Frances and young Mary Elizabeth bake cookies for us to have on Christmas Eve. Their father has devised a neat system for keeping prying fingers out of the cookie jar beforehand. He lettered a sign and put it on the big crock which says:
"God is watching. Ask and you shall receive."
Know something? It works.
We've found that the children want to be trusted. Only occasionally does one of them betray that trust. One Saturday morning Rudy ran upstairs because he smelled smoke very strongly. In one of the little children's rooms he found a stack of cloth diapers ablaze. It certainly didn't set itself on fire so he began to question the children. One by one they all denied knowing anything about it. He called them all together and said, "I won't say any more about it but one day whoever set this fire will have to answer to God. It will be easier if you confess it now and ask forgiveness."

Nothing more was said. A few days later, one of the children came to Rudy and confessed. The acknowledgment of it and asking God's forgiveness brought a real change in that child's life. Forgiving and being forgiven are burden-lifters. We are really set free in a particular way that we may not even be able to understand but it truly works every single time. I recommend it!

Packages arrive daily from so many places—from

various youth groups and churches—from people who have heard us tell our story at religious and social gatherings, places where we're invited to speak and share our beliefs. I know that God delights in all of us who tell of His goodness to His children.

"God inhabits the praises of His people," we are told in the Bible. If only we would tell God more that we love Him. If only we would go to Him for help and guidance. Not "so-and-so says" but "God says." He is the provider.

Oftentimes people have difficulty understanding how we can believe God is providing for us when help comes from the hands of men, women and children who send food, money and gifts for our family.

We believe completely that God puts His thoughts into the hearts of people and leads them to share with others. He said, "It is more blessed to give than to receive" (Acts 20:35). It's harder to receive unless you are sure you are doing His work, then He gives you the grace to receive gracefully. Actually God wants to bless us coming and going!

Every Friday a dear friend, Mary Lanzara, comes to the house with ten pounds of chopped meat, two large pork roasts or a big ham. Harvey Bruen supplies us with bread, rolls and doughnuts every weekend. So many people love us and help us.

When we have a lot of money, we buy a lot of food. When we have a little money, we buy a little food and trust God for what we lack. God is the only one who can take nothing, multiply it and get something.

We see it happen with the distressed ones who come to

A Christmas Celebration

us. They have no love. We give them some of ours, and soon we each have more. God's economic system beats anything man has yet devised. He wants to give us His best. He only wants us to ask.

A certain woman came to me once and said, "God isn't doing the work of looking after all these children. You are."

I answered. "No, Mrs. White. These are God's children and it's His strength that I work through. There's no way I could possibly do it on my own. No way!"

I doubt if she understood but I hope so.

Christmas Eve came at last and we bundled up the children to go to church. Everyone loved the Christmas carols. We had our own sing-along around the piano when we returned home, with Rudy, Jr. at the keyboard and all the voices singing out. The older kids held the younger ones and everybody had a great time for half an hour, then they became restless.

Mary Claire, Mary Christine, Mary Margaret, Matthew, Frankie and Eric decided to check on Lassie and her five new puppies in the laundry room.

Mary Elizabeth and Mary Frances left to wrap packages upstairs. Mary Ann and Mary Grace went to the kitchen to make cocoa. Michael, in his wheelchair, gave the younger ones rides from the living room to the stairway in the main hall where Rudy and I picked them up and took the youngest and sleepiest to bed. They are Jon, Timmy and Marty. Ali and Veronica are in Pennsylvania. Rudy, Jr. is playing the piano.

Michael Joseph, David, Billy and Robert play a quick

game of checkers. Finally, the children are tucked in, kissed and prayed over. Rudy and I then went downstairs, tired after a long, exciting day. Tonight I especially feel the added weight of the new life I'm carrying. I'll be glad when March arrives bringing the new baby.

I collapsed on the couch in the library and kicked off my shoes. Rudy loosened his tie and gratefully sat down. We could hear the girls in the kitchen washing the cups and setting the table for breakfast. Just the two of us alone for the first time in several days. Rudy has a holiday along with the school kids, except he will still keep an eye on the buildings and equipment so that nothing is damaged or frozen while school is not in session.

Rudy stretched out his long legs and relaxed.

"Had a call from the real estate agent this afternoon."

I sat up at once, all excited, expecting to hear some fabulous news. We had put our house on the market, feeling strongly that we were to make another change in our lives. Ali Gonzales, pastor of a nondenominational church in the Philippines, wanted us to come there and help him and his wife organize and run an orphanage. We'd take all our children, live in and help run the place with them. Both Rudy and I felt we should go. Now he was telling me he'd had a call about the house.

"What did they say, Rudy? Did somebody make you an offer?"

"They did. I told them we'd have to pray about it and let them know."

"What was the offer?"

"A hundred and thirty thousand."

A Christmas Celebration

"But that's not the figure we felt God telling us to ask. What do you think we should do?"

"Just what I told the man. Pray about it and let him know."

It's always been thrilling to me to know that I married a man of action. He came over to the couch and knelt down. With my unwieldy shape it was impossible for me to join him on the floor so I just held his hands and prayed along with him.

For about fifteen or twenty minutes we talked to God and asked His guidance. When we finished we both felt He meant for us to wait for the figure He had impressed upon our minds—one hundred fifty thousand dollars. God knows how much we'll need when we get there. When that offer comes in, we'll know it's time to go. It may be that we are meant to stick around here until all the adoption proceedings are finished and the family is complete. Anyway, we had turned it over to God so the problem was no longer ours.

Rudy gathered up the letters and cards that were lying in a basket on the television set, brought them over and sat down beside me.

He patted me on the tummy. "Well, Sarah, it won't be too long now. This time next Christmas we'll have a little Isaac or Jacob."

"Not so fast, Abraham! Those are not the names I've got picked out. Besides, it might be a girl, so there."

Rudy started looking at the Christmas mail he'd put on the coffee table.

"Have you seen all these, Joanne?"

"Haven't had time, honey. Some I've looked at, but not all.

I hope there's a letter in there from Merlyn. Take a look."

We started going through the cards and letters and, sure enough, there was a nice, fat letter from Georgia. I read every single line. Rudy was reading something that looked like a poem. He handed it to me and I noticed how quiet he'd gotten. I read it too. It was a poem, written by one of the men he worked with at Mountain Lakes School System. It was written for Rudy.

BOSS

A man of faith is hard to find,
Who lives each day with God in mind;
And takes on the burdens of those not his,
Yet never gets tired, just gives and gives.

A poor man by nature, yet rich in his joys,
All of his treasures, his girls and his boys;
Not knowing today what tomorrow will bring,
If he happens to worry, he'll start to sing.

How often I've wished to be a man such as he,
He showed me the way, it's easy to see;
Put your whole life in the hands of the Lord,
For He holds unending happiness in store.

Give Him your soul, to do with as He may,
He won't let you down, you need simply pray;
How happy I am to have one such as he,
Not just as a boss, but a father to me.

A Christmas Celebration

How wonderful will be the end of this life,
To be there with Him, with no pain and no strife;
And when the time comes that our Maker we'll see,
I know that He'll smile, when he calls, "Rudy."

I looked at Rudy and saw a tear rolling down his cheek. He was deeply moved by this simple tribute. It wasn't the only poem. There was another one—two letters down in the stack.

"Rudy, here's another poem. I never thought anyone would ever write verses about us, did you? Listen to this."

ANN'S POEM

As I look behind the shadow of time
And now see what I've been missing,
I think of what was never mine,
The Lord, His love, His blessing!

Thank you, Lord, for Rudy, my friend,
And how you spoke through him,
He said don't fret, don't have to worry,
"The Lord will work within."

I'd come to his home, he'd hand me a Book,
And I'd keep it so close to me;
When fear sets in or my heart has a burden,
His little Book sets me free!

I praise you, Lord; I love you, Jesus,
For what you've done for me,
You walked along my rugged road,
And you won my victory!

OUR GROWING FAMILY

It says in Revelation 3:20
That Jesus stands and knocks,
Oh, praise His name, I opened the door
With Joanne and Rudy Sheptock.

By this time we were both crying and could hardly see to read the rest of the mail, some of which was bills—one being a large amount due for car insurance. I heard Rudy saying another prayer as I got the big, brown scrapbook from the desk and slipped the new cards in with dozens of others we had received other months, other years. Some had dates, some didn't, but each told a story of love and generosity.

Rudy's prayer was concluding, "If you want us to start walking that's okay, Lord, but you know we can't meet this insurance payment. We leave it in your hands."

"To the Sheptocks . . . God bless you all. What you are doing for these children is immeasurable. I've enclosed a small gift."

"Please accept this check for use in your home with your growing family. The Lord has led me to make this gift to you and yours for His glory."

February 1976

Dear Friends:
Thank you for being such a good witness to me of how the Lord provides for our every need.

A Christmas Celebration

I was impressed by the newspaper article about your family. It's worth more than all the sermons in the world put together.

Dear Mr. and Mrs. Sheptock:
I hope the enclosed check will help you in the work you are doing with the many children you have taken into your home . . . I, as a member of Alcoholics Anonymous, am in a program which is based on sharing our love and understanding with suffering alcoholics and with all mankind. You are truly living the philosophy of our program and I would be proud to know you.

December 1976

The enclosed check is sent to you to assist you in your work with so many children suffering from various disabilities and handicaps. May God bless you both and your own children. May He strengthen you as you walk the way of faith, and may your example of living be a source of strength to myself as well as to many, many others. God bless all of you.
In the name of Jesus our Lord,
Reverend Monsignor Denis A. Hayes

December 1976

Dear Joanne:
Thanks for the money order. I really needed it when I got it. Thanks again. Love, D.J.

While Rudy was still looking through the current mail, I was engrossed in one letter that stood out from all the rest. It was a note Mary Grace had written us shortly after she'd become our daughter. It was something I could never read without crying.

Dear Mom and Dad:
When you took me into your family and adopted me as your own daughter, you will never know what it meant to me. I knew that this was God's will for my life because of the confirmation of this letter and check which came to me soon after that. Someone sent me a thousand-dollar check anonymously, so that "our Lord Jesus Christ may continue to bless the work you are doing with the strength and encouragement and love He provides."
I give it to you with all my love,
Mary Grace

I closed the scrapbook and got up to turn off the kitchen lights. Two unopened letters fell off the couch as I stood up. Rudy reached for them. The house was so quiet I could hear him tearing the envelopes while I was in the kitchen. In a moment I turned to find him at my elbow. He handed one of the letters to me:

Dear Friends:
God has abundantly blessed and we would like to share this blessing with you via the enclosed check.
Louise and Charlie

A Christmas Celebration

The check was for seven hundred dollars, more than enough to pay the insurance bill. It had arrived in the same mail as the bill but had been kept for us to see at the last.

If our cups were full on Christmas Eve, they were overflowing on Christmas morning. Among the many packages and presents was a clumsily wrapped gift under the tree for Rudy and me: a small, square box that rattled when we opened it. Inside was a note from the children signed, "The Snow Shovelers." In the box was a total of $39.15, money they had made shoveling snow for neighbors.

There's nothing more we can add to our story except to say that God's dividends never cease. On April 10, 1978, He blessed us with the birth of Samuel Joshua Sheptock, weight nine pounds, three ounces, who looks like his brother Matthew and his sister Mary Frances.

He's a beautiful, perfect, dimpled baby boy. The children adore him and love to watch him nurse. Margy remarks in disdain, "I'll bet that's low-fat milk!"

Samuel is a child of God. Jesus said so.

"See how great a love the Father has bestowed upon us, that we should be called the children of God; and such we are" (1 John 3:1).

And so we all are!

15

Love in Bloom

This is the Sheptock story—Rudy and Joanne's "flowers" in full bloom. From the foreword to the very end it was intended to show the sure provision of a loving God.

Joanne and Rudy's words have already encouraged many people, as evidenced by the letters they have received, letters from people who have been helped by the Sheptocks' brokenness, humility and overriding belief in God's goodness.

They wouldn't put it in the story but I know that many times they give out of their own need, to a young girl with many problems, to a church in the Philippines, to many others in trouble. Why? Because they truly believe we are meant to love one another with everything we have.

I owe a debt of gratitude to every child in the Sheptock family, natural, adopted and unadopted, for they have opened my eyes to a new world. I love them all.

Also I owe many thanks to people who have read the manuscript, made suggestions, offered help and prayer. I'd especially like to include Sr. Marguerite Francis Goodwin and Sr. Mary Ellen Gleason of the Sisters of

Charity, Convent Station, New Jersey. Their *Caritas* yearbook was invaluable. Thanks also to Dorothy Brennan, Rita Salm, Liz Henderson and May Baker for their special helps.

To the men of the *USS Stoddard*, my appreciation for the handsome pictorial logbook that captured so fully the very essence of life at sea.

Marc Asher's Mother's Day photo of the Sheptock family (from the *Somerset Messenger-Gazette*, May, 1978) was both a delight and an inspiration.

So all of us together have brought forth a story with love and a happy ending. I believe we will all learn something from these children. God has chosen them for a two-fold purpose. One, to reveal to us that we are also crippled, blind and handicapped some of the time. The day that I couldn't accomplish anything for myself or anyone else because I was in a valley of despair, was a day in which my arms were useless. I might as well have had no arms, for all the good I did.

I was also blind. Blind to my neighbor's need, blind to God's love and forgiveness, blind to my own faults.

Having healthy limbs, we are nevertheless crippled when we are unable to reach out and help a brother or to stoop and lift up a child.

Sometimes we are deformed, not nice to look at, because the Spirit Jesus has given us is occluded, cannot be seen through the veil of darkness we hide behind. That is one way God is letting these children serve Him. To remind us that having eyes, we do not always see; having ears, we do not hear.

The other way is this: In a real sense the Sheptock

children are sacrificial lambs, showing us the true Lamb of God. In circumstances of illness and handicaps, not of their own choosing, but because of God's choice, they are becoming little Christs for Him. And oh, the blessings stored up in heaven for them. They will be first in the kingdom, never doubt. For the kingdom of heaven is of such of these.

According to the standards of the world, the Sheptocks are foolish, for their family is constantly expanding. Since the beginning of the story many postscripts have been added.

"Don't you know when to stop?" someone asked not long ago.

They will stop when God tells them to stop, Rudy and Joanne affirm. In the meantime little people like a four-month-old baby will come, and big people, like the two young adults who were in trouble, alone and had no place to turn.

Three other young ones have come in for a four-day stay so their mother can get away for a while. She didn't know Joanne and Rudy but knew of their love for children so she asked if the children might come.

"And whoever receives one such child in my name, receives Me" Jesus said (Luke 9:48).

The Sheptocks would like the book to be dedicated to "Jesus, the author and finisher of our faith. We praise Him, bless Him, love Him and worship Him. We thank Him for dying on the cross for us, for His unconditional love. That it is 'by grace you have been saved through faith; and that not of yourselves, it is the gift of God; not as a result of works, that no one should boast' " (Eph. 2:8, 9).

The Sheptocks' house is the Father's house and in His house are many rooms. There God allows them the privilege of caring for His children, for they too are made to the praise of His glory.

"Do not fear, for I am with you;
I will bring your offspring from the east,
And gather you from the west.
"I will say to the north, 'Give them up!'
And to the south, 'Do not hold them back.'
Bring My sons from afar,
And My daughters from the ends of the earth,
Every one who is called by My name,
And whom I have created for My glory,
Whom I have formed, even whom I have made."
Bring out the people who are blind, even
though they have eyes,
And the deaf, even though they have ears.
(Isa. 43:5-8)